SAINT FRANCES OF HOLLYWOOD

SAINT FRANCES of HOLLYWOOD

A Play in Two Acts
by
SALLY CLARK

Talonbooks
1996

Published with the assistance of the Canada Council.

Talonbooks
#104—3100 Production Way
Burnaby, B.C. V5A 4R4 Canada

Typeset in New Baskerville, Monotone and Mekanik, and
printed and bound in Canada by Hignell Printing.

First Printing: September, 1996

SHAIN JAFFE. (416) 925-2051

Canadian Cataloguing in Publication Data

Clark, Sally, 1953-
    Saint Frances of Hollywood

    A play.
    ISBN 0-88922-366-1

    I. Title.
PS8555.L37197S24 1996   C812'.54   C96-910507-X
PR9199.3.C5235S24 1996

Playwright's Acknowledgements

In 1984, I was possessed by the idea that Frances Farmer's life was a perfect example of a classical tragedy so I decided that I would try and write one.

The Canada Council awarded me a "B" grant to work on *Saint Frances of Hollywood*. It was given a workshop and public reading, directed by Meg Westley at the Stratford Festival in 1986. In 1987, Mary Vingoe directed a workshop and a staged reading at Nightwood Theatre's *Groundswell Festival*. In 1989, I rewrote the script, under the dramaturgical guidance of Robert Rooney, while I was at the Banff Playwright's Colony. It was given a workshop production at Playwright's Workshop in Montreal in March 1993, directed by Glynis Leyshon and later produced at Alberta Theatre Projects' *playRites '94*.

I would like to thank Karl Siegler whose brilliant insight and advice helped me to finally figure out what was wrong with the play. I did my final rewrite and this version was given a public workshop presentation at the University of Cincinnati in November, 1995. It was produced in Toronto in January, 1996.

I would like to thank all the actors who have appeared in the various incarnations of *Saint Frances of Hollywood*. I also wish to thank: Clarke Rogers, Elliott Hayes, Camille Mitchell, Duncan McIntosh, John Murrell, Michelin Chevrier, Daniel Libman, Penn Kemp, Hrant Alianak and Norma Jenckes for their invaluable contributions.

I would like to thank the Canada Council and the Laidlaw Foundation for their support of the play in its early stages. I would like to thank the Ontario Arts Council, the Toronto Arts Council and the Metro Arts Council for their generous financial support which enabled me to produce the play in January, 1996.

Note

"Saint Frances of Hollywood" is not an ironic title. Nowadays, we think of saints as kind gentle souls; "saintlike" implying a serenity that is in itself, miraculous. But there is an older tradition of saints as obnoxious strong-minded rabble rousers who battle against authority in order to serve their cause. These saints were punished for their insubordination. They were tortured to death. They were burned at the stake. To the end, they did not betray their convictions. I believe Frances Farmer to be an unrecognized saint of the 20th century. Frances Farmer defied the authorities of her time. She, too, was tortured but would not recant. Her life itself was extraordinary, encompassing the primary obsessions of the 20th century—aetheism, Communism, media manipulation and psychiatry. Frances Farmer was a legend at Steilacoom. She organized the patients of Ward D and set them in rebellion against the authorities. Nurses who worked there spoke of a strange power emanating from her.

I have an early memory of watching *This Is Your Life* when Frances Farmer was the featured guest. I remember being frightened by this confused but recalcitrant woman who could not remember her life and what is more, did not want to. Even as a lobotomized guest, Frances Farmer managed to be subversive. I have never felt the same way about television since.

This published version of **Saint Frances of Hollywood** was first produced by Hollywood Ten in association with Independent Artists Productions and Canadian Rep Theatre at The Canadian Stage Theatre in Toronto, Ontario on January 17, 1996 with the following cast:

Thea Gill *as Frances Farmer*

Allan Aarons	Jack Nicholsen
Martha Gibson	George Sperdakos
Kate Lynch	Peter Van Wart
Jennifer Doyle	Jason Jones
Eliza-Jane Scott	Christopher Robertson

Directed by Hrant Alianak
Set Design by Adam Swica
Models by Randy Gledhill
Light & Video Design: Chris Clifford
Costume Design: Angela Elter
Sound by Jack Nicholsen
Stage Manger: April A. Nicolle

An earlier version of **Saint Frances of Hollywood** was first produced by Alberta Theatre Projects, D. Michael Dobbin, Producing Director, as part of playRites '94 sponsored in part by Shell Canada Ltd., in February, 1994 with the following cast:

Megan Leitch *as Frances Farmer*

Joyce Campion	Robert Benson
Marianne Copithorne	Neil Barclay
Gina Wilkinson	Chris Mackie
Christopher Hunt	

Directed by Charlotte Lee
Concept Consultant: Glynis Leyshon
Set Design: John Dinning
Costume Design: Carolyn Smith
Lighting Design: Harry Frehner
Composer: Allan Rae
Stage Managers: Charlotte Green, Dianne Goodman,
& Rose Brow

CAST OF CHARACTERS

FRANCES FARMER
LILLIAN FARMER, *her mother*
ERNEST FARMER, *her father*
RALPH SCHWAB, *an agent*
BILL ANDERSON, *Frances' husband*
JUDGE FRATER
LOUELLA PARSONS, *gossip columnist*

CLIFFORD ODETS	ROY DICKSELL
HAROLD CLURMAN	BELLE MACKENZIE
LUISE (MRS. ODETS)	JEAN
GLORIA GARNET	MAN 1
EDNA BURGE	MAN 2
DR. SWAN	WOMAN 1
DR. NICHOLSON	DIRECTOR
DR. BETELGEUSE	ACTOR
MISS CARLYLE	2 POLICEMEN
GORDO	NURSE
GORDO'S FRIEND	MATRON
DR. WALTER FREEMAN	ORDERLY
ALFRED KNOBBLE	ATTENDANTS
MAN IN HOTEL	

1 actress	Frances Farmer
1 acress	Lillian/Jean
1 actress	Louella Parsons/Miss Carlyle/
	Gloria Garnet/Nurse in Sanitorium
1 actress	Mrs. Odets/Edna Burge/
	Nurse in Steilacoom
1 actor	Odets/Dr.Freeman
1 actor	Bill/ Dr. Swan
1 actor	Dr. Betelgeuse/Alfred Knobble
1 actor	Dr. Nicholson

With the exception of the doubling roles of Lillian/Jean and Odets/Freeman, the roles can be juggled amongst the actors. For example, Edna Burge could be played by a male actor. The Nurses and Matron could also be played by men.

The running time of Saint Frances of Hollywood is:
Act One: 60-65 minutes; Act Two: 45-50 minutes.

Act One

SCENE 1

A drunken woman (FRANCES FARMER) lies sprawled on the ground. With difficulty, she props herself up.

FRANCES:
Everyone knows the story about the American Indian who wouldn't have his picture taken because he believed his soul would be stolen from him and captured forever in that little box. Everyone laughs and thinks how quaint. How superstitious. *(slight pause)* But what if it's true? What if each time your picture is taken you lose a tiny piece of what defines you? I make a film and some flickering part of me is caught and refracted into a million particles. It's there on the screen but it isn't inside me, anymore. It lies there, glimmering, imprisoned on some white backdrop. It's left me. My light has been stolen.

Sound of a film projector. Lights up on a huge filmed soundless close-up of Frances Farmer in all her glory on a screen above the drunken woman.

Blackout.

NOTE:
This should be the only blackout in this play. The scenes should be directed to flow smoothly from one to another.

SCENE 2

FRANCES, age 16, alone on stage.

FRANCES:
When I was a little girl, my mother said that I was an angel
sent by God. I thought this was probably true because I
would ask God for things and I would get them. One day, I
lost my hat. I asked God to find it for me. Sure enough,
He did. But then, that same day, my best friend, Clara, lost
both her parents in a car crash. Initially, I blamed myself. I
thought God was too busy looking for my hat to take care
of Clara's parents. Then, it struck me.

*Lights change. FRANCES reads from a paper. LILLIAN, her
mother, enters and listens.*

FRANCES:
If God loved all his children equally, why did He bother
about my hat and let other children lose their fathers and
mothers for always. I began to see that He didn't have
much to do with people's dying or hats or anything. Life
was one large accident but if you really concentrated, you
could guide certain events in your favour. My faith in God
was actually just me exercising my will. I felt rather proud
to think that I had found the truth by myself, without help
from anyone. God was gone.

LILLIAN:
Francie, that's wonderful!

FRANCES:
Really, Mamma?

LILLIAN:
You're blessed, Francie. You're marked for great things.

10

FRANCES:
My teacher, Mrs. Mackenzie, wants to print it in the paper. She says everyone's going to be up in arms.

LILLIAN:
I know you still believe in God and that's what's important.

FRANCES:
But that's just it, Mamma. I don't—

LILLIAN:
God has put you on this earth and He has given you special gifts to do his work.

FRANCES:
But that would mean that some people are more important than others. I thought God was supposed to love everyone equally.

LILLIAN:
He does. Just not for reasons that we can see. Now, your point about free will is interesting. I've often wondered why I haven't been more successful in life. I have the will for it.

FRANCES:
But Mamma, you are successful. You created a whole new bird.

LILLIAN:
That's true. Crossing a turkey with a hen wasn't easy but I did it. Bird Americana. Red, white and blue. The works. Do you think the President will like it?

FRANCES:
You should probably write before you send it. Just so he won't be too surprised.

LILLIAN:

    I guess so. You have to think big if you want to get ahead, Francie. Wouldn't you like to go to Washington some day?

FRANCES:

    I'd like to go all around the world, Mamma.

LILLIAN:

    (laughs) I don't know how but I know you'll do it if you set your mind to it. Use your will when you're young and strong. I lost mine when I married your father. But I got it back the day I had you. You'll be famous one day, Francie. I can feel it in my bones.

FRANCES:

    Really, Mamma?

LILLIAN:

    You want to be famous, don't you?

FRANCES:

    (nods)

LILLIAN:

    I'm the only one who understands you. I know your soul, little sister.

FRANCES:

    Do you, Mamma? Do you really?

SCENE 3

FRANCES and her father, ERNEST.

ERNEST:
Have you told your mother?

FRANCES:
She hasn't come home yet.

ERNEST:
It's going to play havoc with her blood pressure. You have the strangest luck.

FRANCES:
It's not luck, Dad. It's no accident that I won the contest. I willed it to happen.

ERNEST:
You did?

FRANCES:
Yes.

ERNEST:
Do you often will things to happen?

FRANCES:
Just the things I want.

ERNEST:
Like what?

FRANCES:
Well, I want to work with Clifford Odets and The Group Theatre in New York. Hollywood's a possibility but from what I've read—they have no integrity.

ERNEST:
> You really think you can get anything you want?

FRANCES:
> Well, how do you explain the fact that one of my dreams
> has come true already.

ERNEST:
> *(baffled)* I can't.

> *LILLIAN enters.*

LILLIAN:
> Francie! Ernie! You'll never guess what's happened! A
> Hollywood talent scout was at Francie's school play last
> night. And guess what!

FRANCES:
> What?

LILLIAN:
> *(as though imparting the wisdom of the ages)*
> He said you had "It."

ERNEST:
> It?

LILLIAN:
> Yes. "It!" Isn't that exciting!

ERNEST:
> Does that mean something?

LILLIAN:
> IT! Of course, it means something! If you stopped drink-
> ing, we might be able to save some money and send our
> daughter to Hollywood.

ERNEST:
Thanks for reminding me. *(gets up and pours himself a Scotch)*

FRANCES:
Mamma, I—ah—won a free trip, today.

LILLIAN:
To Hollywood!! Oh! That's so exciting!

FRANCES:
Ah—no, Mamma. To Russia.

LILLIAN:
What?

FRANCES:
I'm going to Russia. I leave next week. Isn't that exciting!

LILLIAN:
WHAT!

FRANCES:
My theatre group had a subscription drive for the 'Voice of Action' newspaper and my name was—

LILLIAN:
That's a Communist paper.

ERNEST:
Now now, Lil—

FRANCES:
No, Mamma, it's Socialist and—

LILLIAN:
AAAAGH!

ERNEST:
Breathe Lil, just breathe.

FRANCES:
Calm down, Mamma. I was chosen to represent American youth. First I go to New York. I'm hoping to meet the Group Theatre.

LILLIAN:
Oh God! More Communists!

FRANCES:
Socialists, Mamma.

LILLIAN:
I can't have you consorting with a bunch of Reds.

FRANCES:
I have to go! It's my only chance to get out of here.

LILLIAN:
You don't like your home?!

FRANCES:
Of course I love my home.

ERNEST:
I don't.

LILLIAN:
(to ERNEST) You stay out of it! *(to FRANCES)* You'll start spouting Commie propaganda—

FRANCES:
But Mamma, it has nothing to do with Communism!

ERNEST:
Let her go, Lil, she'll never have another opportunity like this one.

LILLIAN:
I know Commies. They'll hypnotize her and make her one of their own! When she comes back—IF she comes back, she'll be put on the Black List.

ERNEST:
For God's sake, Lil, Frannie's only 19. They don't blacklist children.

LILLIAN:
(to FRANCES) You're not going and that's final!

FRANCES:
I'm sorry, Mamma, but I am going and you can't stop me! *(leaves)*

LILLIAN:
(shouts after her) You'll go to Hell! You'll go straight to Hell!

SCENE 4

Back from Russia. New York.

FRANCES:
(announces) I have seen the world and now I am ready to make my mark on it.

FRANCES talks to a small group of people at a party.

FRANCES:
They are trying to change the way we live. No one owns anything in Russia. Everything is shared. There's no separation between people. A classless society.

MAN 1:
There's a class system all right. They've simply replaced the aristocracy with a bunch of greedy political thugs.

FRANCES:
That's not what I saw. People in high positions lived very simply.

WOMAN 1:
Did you see Stalin's home?

FRANCES:
Well, no, of course not. But the local commissars invited me to their homes. I saw the factories, the farms—everyone working at what they're good at. No unemployment, no bread line-ups—

MAN 1:
Bet the food's terrible.

FRANCES:
It was simple. But everyone got to eat. Take life in America—what do you do about the fact that some people wear furs and travel in chauffeured limousines while other people starve to death.

WOMAN 1:
I give my money to charity.

FRANCES:
It's not working though, is it? The Soviet system has flaws but at least they are trying to redress the balance between the rich and the poor.

A man (CLIFFORD ODETS) enters into the conversation.

ODETS:
The poor are poor because they're lazy. Why should we subsidize people who won't work?

FRANCES:
There's no chance here for the poor to get work.

ODETS:
Communism will fail because it goes against human nature. All men are not created equal and it's ridiculous to build an entire society around that premise.

FRANCES:
So what's your premise?

ODETS:
The brilliant shall lead, the stupid shall follow.

FRANCES:
Well then, you're in trouble, aren't you?

ODETS:
No need to be rude. It's a natural law—survival of the fittest. Free enterprise.

FRANCES:
Yes and who can forget that monument to free enterprise—the Stock Market Crash. I suppose you did quite well on that?

ODETS:
Just how old do you think I am?

MAN 1 and WOMAN 1 get embarrassed and leave.

ODETS:
My goodness, you're quite a ferocious little girl when you get going.

FRANCES
I'm not a little girl.

ODETS:
No. That's apparent. You're not. I'm sorry. I was baiting you. Devil's Advocate. It's a terrible habit.

FRANCES:
It's a stupid habit. Why do you argue over things you don't believe in?

ODETS:
I'm a playwright. Debating's always a useful exercise for dialogue.

FRANCES:
Well, I'm glad I've been of use to you. *(turns to leave)*

ODETS:
Don't leave. You're so passionate about everything. You're the most breathtaking woman I've ever laid eyes on.

FRANCES:
(smiles) Don't overdo it.

ODETS:
A safe topic, then. The theatre in Russia. How was 'The Seagull?'

FRANCES:
How did you know I'd seen it?

ODETS
Well, you'd have to. You're Nina.

FRANCES:
She goes mad.

ODETS:
Yes, that is a bit of a disappointment. But she's fiery and passionate and beautiful.

FRANCES:
And do you see yourself as Trigorin?

ODETS:
Yes.

FRANCES:
A second-rate writer.

ODETS:
Yes, that's a bit of a disappointment as well. He's second-rate and she goes mad. We'll have to do better than that. *(takes her hand in a seductive manner)*

> *A MAN, standing off to one side, bellows at ODETS.*

MAN 2:
CLIFF! Where have you been! We need you!

ODETS:
Christ, I forgot! *(turns to FRANCES)* I have to leave you. Sorry. *(leaves)*

> *FRANCES' agent (RALPH SCHWAB) rushes up to her as ODETS leaves.*

RALPH:
Frances, I'm glad I tracked you down.

FRANCES:
Who is that man?

RALPH:
You don't know?!

FRANCES:
No. Who is he?

RALPH:
Geez, Frances, that's Clifford Odets.

FRANCES:
Oh my God! That's him?

RALPH:
Yeah, now listen, a goddamn miracle has just happened!

FRANCES:
(dreamily) Yes.

RALPH:
I got you a screen test!

FRANCES:
The things I said—

RALPH:
Some scout saw your audition—thinks you're the next Garbo.

FRANCES:
I'm so embarrassed.

RALPH:
Embarrassed? Whydja be embarrassed? You leave tomorrow.

FRANCES:
What?

RALPH:
For Hollywood. You leave tomorrow.

FRANCES:
Ralph, I just met Clifford Odets. I'm going to stay here
and see if I can work with the Group.

RALPH:
Are you crazy? People work here for years—praying to be
in a hit play so that some bozo from Hollywood will
"discover" them. Everybody wants to be in the movies.

FRANCES:
But I don't care about the movies. I want to work with The
Group.

RALPH:
They're not gonna let you in just like that. Maybe Odets
liked you but ya gotta contend with the rest of them and
they're pretty tight. Look, go to Hollywood, make a name
for yourself and then join the Group. They'll like you
better if you've got money.

FRANCES:
You don't understand. The Group Theatre isn't about
money. You can't pay to join them. I want to do something
important with my life. Being in movies is so frivolous.

RALPH:
I know, I know, ya wanna help people. Well, movies can
help people. Take 'City Lights.' That movie helped a lot of
blind people.

FRANCES:
Only the ones who saw it.

RALPH:

Exactly! Just go for the screen test. If you bomb, you can always come back here. And if it goes well, you could be a Star! What can you lose?

FRANCES:

It's funny. My Mamma always wanted me to go to Hollywood. She hasn't spoken to me since I went to Russia. This would make her very happy.

RALPH:

Then do it for your Mamma. Make her happy.

FRANCES:

For my Mamma! *(takes his hand)*

SCENE 5

SCREEN TEST.

Film crew bustling about. FRANCES sees the MALE ACTOR she is to do the scene with.

FRANCES:
  (goes up to him) Hi, I'm Frances Farmer. Do you want to rehearse our lines together?

ACTOR:
  You don't have lines, do you?

FRANCES:
  I have a few.

ACTOR:
  Not enough to waste my time on. It's not your screen test.

FRANCES:
  I was under the impression that we were both being tested.

ACTOR:
  Oh la de da, "I was under the impression—" you're a real little lady, aren't you. They aren't interested in you, doll. It's me they're after. I'm gonna be playing the lead in some jungle movie.

FRANCES:
  Really?

ACTOR:
  Yeah. *(moves away)* Now, I gotta get into character. I'll do what I do best and you do what you do best. Just stand there and look beautiful. *(leaves)*

DIRECTOR:
  OKAY EVERYONE! TAKE YOUR PLACES!

25

The MALE ACTOR stands in front of the camera.
FRANCES stands off to one side.

DIRECTOR:
ACTION!

ACTOR:
(turns and looks) My God! It's you!

FRANCES:
Yes.

> *Camera turns briefly to FRANCES, then focuses back on the*
> *man.*

ACTOR:
Get away from me! I can't bear to be near you! *(turns away*
from FRANCES)

FRANCES:
(enters his "Frame" by grabbing him and spinning him around)
Look at me, you fool!

ACTOR:
What? Hey! She's not supposed to—

FRANCES:
Do you think I've come all the way from New York just to
stand here and do nothing!

ACTOR:
What? Now, wait a minute. THIS IS MY SCREEN TEST!

FRANCES:
You killed your wife, Tom!

ACTOR:
What!

DIRECTOR:
Keep rolling.

ACTOR:
I did not! *(acting)* HOW DARE YOU ACCUSE ME OF
SUCH THINGS! YOU SCHEMING LITTLE FLOOZY!

FRANCES:
I was afraid you might hate me. Every night I dream that
you are looking at me and don't recognize me. If only you
knew! Ever since I arrived I've been walking here...by the
lake.

ACTOR:
GET THE HELL OUT OF MY SCREEN TEST, YOU
BITCH!

DIRECTOR:
CUT! *(to FRANCES)* What's that last part from?

FRANCES:
A play. 'The Seagull.'

DIRECTOR:
Do you know any more?

FRANCES:
Oh yes.

ACTOR:
What about me!

DIRECTOR:
Oh, sorry. Thanks for coming, Tom.

ACTOR:
Robert! My name's Robert!

DIRECTOR:
We'll call you. *(to FRANCES)* Can you do a little more?

FRANCES:
(nods)

DIRECTOR:
Roll it!

FRANCES:
(waits for camera to frame her face) "For the happiness of being a writer or an actress, I would endure poverty, disillusionment, the hatred of my family; I would live in a garret and eat black bread, suffer dissatisfactions with myself and the recognition of my own imperfections, but in return, I should demand fame...real, resounding fame..."

SCENE 6

Studio. Dance class for actors. FRANCES and BILL and a group of others are hopping up and down, doing dance-like routines.

TEACHER:
  BREAK!

> *The actors disperse into small clusters. FRANCES and BILL are downstage.*

BILL:
  Boy, they really keep us on the hop.

FRANCES:
  Literally.

BILL:
  Thor!

FRANCES:
  What?

BILL:
  What do you think? Thor Anderson.

FRANCES:
  Thor Anderson?

BILL:
  Bill's so boring. I'm not getting anywhere.

FRANCES:
  Changing your name isn't going to fix it.

BILL:
  Don't get onto that willpower stuff. It doesn't work for me. Though there is one thing I want. And I'm concentrating real hard.

FRANCES:
Bill!

TEACHER:
(announces) Partners—please! Today, the Tango.*

> *It doesn't have to be the Tango. Any dance popular in 1933
> that is flirtatious will be a good choice.

> Dance music starts up. FRANCES and BILL are partners.
> The other people partner up. BILL is a very good dancer.

BILL:
Well, why not?

FRANCES:
I feel I've known you all my life but shouldn't we wait?

BILL:
Why? I'm nuts about you, Frances. We're together all the
time, anyway.

FRANCES:
But what happens when we're not sharing our lives. When
you're doing one film and I'm in another.

BILL:
Why would it be different?

FRANCES:
Could we talk to each other so easily then?

BILL:
Sure, why not?

FRANCES:
There's one thing that worries me.

BILL:
What?

FRANCES:
How many times have you read 'Moby Dick?'

BILL:
Three. Are you going to start on that again?

FRANCES:
And how many other books have you read?

BILL:
What's your problem?

FRANCES:
It's the only book you've read!

BILL:
It's the only book you need to read.

FRANCES:
There! That's it! We have totally different philosophies to life.

BILL:
You won't marry me because I like 'Moby Dick?'

FRANCES:
You find one good thing and you stick with it. I like to try everything.

BILL:
You want to sleep around?

FRANCES:
No, of course not. You always take things so literally. Philosophically, I need to explore.

BILL:
You're too up in the air, Frances. That's why you need me. I'll bring you down to earth. Marriage isn't about two people being exactly the same. It's about two people making a whole. We fit, you 'n me. *(pulls her towards him)* Come on, you know you're nuts about me.

FRANCES:
Mmmhmmm.

BILL:
And I'm nuts about you. How bout it?

FRANCES:
(flirtatiously, imitating a cheap floozy) Whaddya think I am? Fast!

BILL:
You bet! *(spins FRANCES up in the air in a special dance flourish)*

SCENE 7

Seattle. The Bijou Theatre. FRANCES, BILL, LILLIAN and ERNEST stand outside.

LILLIAN:
Oh, I'm so excited, Francie. Your first film. And it's here at the Bijou.

ERNEST:
Are you in this film too, Bill?

BILL:
No. But I'll be in one soon, won't I, doll?

FRANCES:
Yes. Bill's up for a western.

BILL:
"Up" for it?! I got it! It's in the bag, doll.

FRANCES:
Do we have to stand here and greet people?

ERNEST:
Yes. I feel somewhat conspicuous.

LILLIAN:
You can go and sit down, Ernie, but I promised Marge. It's a big night for her. *(to FRANCES)* You know, she wanted you to wear your usherette uniform.

FRANCES:
(laughs) Really? I should have done that.

LILLIAN:
I told her where to get off. Where's your tiara?

BILL:
Yeah, she looks great in it. A real princess. She wore it
when we got married. Course—she didn't know she was
wearing it *(snickers)*

FRANCES:
Bill...

LILLIAN:
I would have loved to have been there.

FRANCES:
Mamma—

BILL:
Blame me, Mrs. Farmer. I got her pissed one night and
scooted her off to a chapel in Las Vegas. I didn't know
Frances had parents.

LILLIAN:
Really?

BILL:
Uh—sorry. She just never talked about you guys.

FRANCES:
Bill...

BILL:
Yeah. Sorry, Mrs. Farmer. You're swell, ya know. You 'n
Ernie. You're just swell.

LILLIAN:
Swell. Put your tiara on, dear.

FRANCES:
Mamma, I can't wear that tiara. It's really stupid-looking.
I'm overdressed as it is. It's just a movie.

BILL:
Just a movie! If I got a movie like that, I'd be laughing.

LILLIAN:
You're a star. You're a big star.

FRANCES:
Sssh, Mamma.

LILLIAN:
Do you have to go back tomorrow morning? I've arranged press interviews. *(sees someone coming)* Oh my God! Judge Frater!

ERNEST:
Your ally in the war against Communism.

LILLIAN:
That's an old subject, Ernest. Frances has changed now.

FRANCES:
Who says I've—

Judge Frater arrives.

FRATER:
Mrs. Farmer, a pleasure. Mr. Farmer. And your charming daughter. *(to LILLIAN)* My my, you must be very proud of her.

LILLIAN:
I certainly am. This is Frances' husband, Bill Anderson.

BILL:
Wycliffe.

LILLIAN:
Pardon?

BILL:
Wycliffe Anderson. How'd ja do? *(grabs FRATER's hand and shakes it vigorously)*

FRATER:
(puzzled) Pleasure. *(pause)*You know, Frances, your mother and I were quite worried about you a few years ago.

FRANCES:
Yes. I remember. You used to hate me. You called me the "Little Red."

FRATER:
Well, that's all water under the bridge.

FRANCES:
You didn't like my saying that God was dead, either.

FRATER:
God isn't dead!

BILL:
You said God was dead?! Geez!

FRATER:
(laughs tensely) That was a long time ago. Now, you're all grown up and absolutely ravishing.

FRANCES:
Why are we going through this facade?

LILLIAN:
Francie, make nice.

FRANCES:
Make nice. Why? The sheer hypocrisy of it all. *(puts tiara on)* God is dead and the Government stinks. *(points to tiara)* Does this make it all better?

LILLIAN:
FRANCES!

FRATER:
WELL!

ERNEST:
You'll have to excuse my daughter, your Honour. She hates
hypocrites.

LILLIAN:
ERNIE!

ERNEST:
Uh—oh, sorry, your Honour. I didn't mean to imply that
you were a hypocrite. Just that my daughter might have
thought—

FRATER:
I didn't come here to be insulted! *(leaves)*

    ERNEST and FRANCES burst into fits of laughter.

FRANCES:
That was brilliant, Dad!

BILL:
I'm a little confused. What the hell happened just then?

LILLIAN:
Now you've really done it! (*to ERNEST)* You've just kissed
what remains of your law career goodbye. *(to FRANCES)*
And you! Why can't you behave?! Would it have killed you
to have been nice to him?

FRANCES:
He's always hated me, Mamma. Why should we pretend
otherwise. He's just a pompous old fart.

LILLIAN:
You shouldn't underestimate a man like that. You've just made a powerful enemy. He rules this town.

FRANCES:
Well, I'll just make sure I stay out of Seattle.

LILLIAN:
But we've hardly spent any time together at all. I'll come back to Hollywood with you.

FRANCES:
But Mamma, I'm on the set every day. It wouldn't be much fun for you. Besides, what would Dad do without you?

ERNEST:
I'd be fine.

LILLIAN:
You just don't want me to come!

FRANCES:
Of course, you can come, Mamma.

LILLIAN:
And I can stay with you?

FRANCES and BILL exchange a look.

BILL:
Sure, Mrs. Farmer, that'd be swell.

LILLIAN:
Oh! *(hugs FRANCES)* You've made me so happy! I'll help you. I'll be your agent.

FRANCES:
I already have an agent, Mamma.

LILLIAN:
I can help him. You're gonna be famous, little sister. All over this country, they'll be saying your name.

SCENE 8

Hollywood. A street. CLIFFORD ODETS and FRANCES FARMER. FRANCES walks past CLIFFORD ODETS. She does not see him.

ODETS:
Frances Farmer!

FRANCES:
(spins around, is surprised) Mr. Odets?

ODETS:
My little Nina. I never knew your name. You vanished like a thief in the night.

FRANCES:
You vanished, actually.

ODETS:
Women! Why do they have such accurate memories. I scoured New York looking for you. Not a trace. It was as though you'd disappeared from the face of the earth.

FRANCES:
The earth as we know it. I came to Hollywood.

ODETS:
Yes, yes. I saw that film, 'Get Out and Scram!'

FRANCES:
'Come and Get It.'

ODETS:
Right. 'Come and Get It.' And there you were. Glittering like a small jewel. My Nina. Amazing the strange turns life takes. You could have been slogging away in some dingy theatre with the rest of us but you escaped that dire fate. And lucky for you, too. Who needs the Group Theatre when your light can be seen all over America.

FRANCES:
You wanted me to join The Group?

ODETS:
Well, yes. Of course, it would have taken some time to
work you in—

FRANCES:
This is amazing! I've dreamed all my life of working with
The Group. I wanted to stay but my agent made me leave
and—

ODETS:
You should never abandon your dreams, Frances.

FRANCES:
I didn't think it was possible.

ODETS:
Anything's possible. It's not too late.

FRANCES:
Pardon?

ODETS:
We're doing my play, 'Golden Boy' this summer. All the
time I was writing it, I couldn't get you out of my mind.
You are the essence of Lorna Moon.

FRANCES:
Lorna Moon?

ODETS:
The woman I'm currently in love with.

FRANCES:
Oh.

ODETS:
One of my characters.

FRANCES:
You do get involved.

ODETS:
Something in you—a stubbornness, a willfulness—has haunted me. You are the only woman in the world who can play this role.

FRANCES:
I—ah—

ODETS:
But that's my foolishness. You've signed your life away. Joined the nunnery.

FRANCES:
Nunnery?

ODETS:
The starlet convent in Hollywood. They've shaved your beautiful strong eyebrows—vow of obedience.

FRANCES:
I've never been very obedient.

ODETS:
But you are under a strict contract, aren't you?

FRANCES:
I might be able to persuade the Studio to give me a few months off. Would there be a part for my husband?

ODETS:
Your husband?

FRANCES:
Yes.

ODETS:
I really did miss the boat, didn't I? No. There is no part for
your husband in my play. Would you come anyway? A
blistering hot summer in New York?

FRANCES:
Sounds enchanting. *(pause)* Yes. I'll do it. I'll ask the Studio
to give me the time off.

ODETS:
You'd do it? For me?! *(kisses her)*

They both look surprised.

ODETS:
Sorry, got carried away.

FRANCES:
Oh—it's um—all right.

*They leave in opposite directions, looking back after each
other.*

SCENE 9

FRANCES and her agent, RALPH SCHWAB.

RALPH:
> You want to WHAT?!

FRANCES:
> Go to New York and do 'Golden Boy.'

RALPH:
> A play?! A play! You want to do a play?! Are you crazy!
> There's this big juicy part in this movie this summer. It's
> Garbo material and the Studio wants you!

FRANCES:
> I have to do this. You promised I could go back. It's only
> for a couple of months.

RALPH:
> There's no point arguing with you. I'll try and keep the
> Studio wolf from the door but you gotta do something for
> me.

FRANCES:
> What?

RALPH:
> Get your mother off my back. She's camped out in my
> office, telling me what to do all day.

FRANCES:
> They banned her from the set. I can't persuade her to go
> back to Seattle.

RALPH:
> The town probably won't let her back in. Oh yeah, clean
> your house. Louella Parsons is doing an Exclusive on you,
> tomorrow. When are you going to move, anyway? It's such
> a shack.

FRANCES:
I don't want a fancy home.

RALPH:
You're a star. You should live like one. And pullease, drop that migrant worker routine.

FRANCES:
What?

RALPH:
You went to one of their rallies. I heard about it. Shit like that doesn't go down well here.

FRANCES:
You and I will never see eye to eye, Ralph.

RALPH:
I know, I know. I'm asking for the world.

LILLIAN FARMER bursts in.

LILLIAN:
There you are, Frances. I was looking all over for you. *(to RALPH)* Why didn't you tell me she was here!

SCENE 10

FRANCES' home in Hollywood. BILL paces back and forth.
He is angry.

BILL:

Great! Just great! Don't even tell me! I have to hear about it through the old battle-axe. When the hell is she going to leave? She's driving me up the frigging wall.

FRANCES:

Soon, Bill. I'm sorry she got to you before I did. I was going to tell you.

BILL:

Tell me. That's what I mean. You tell me stuff. You never ask me.

FRANCES:

Do I need your permission? Please Bill, may I go to New York? Thank you, Bill. Please Bill, may I do this play?

BILL:

All right! I'm sorry. I just wish you'd confide in me more.

FRANCES:

I'm sorry, Bill. Things happen so fast. Would you mind spending a summer in New York?

BILL:

I guess not. What if I get a film here?

FRANCES:

Then we'll be apart for a while.

The doorbell rings.

FRANCES:

Oh my God! Louella Parsons!

BILL:
Louella Parsons?! She's interviewing you?! And you didn't tell me!

FRANCES:
I meant to.

BILL:
Yeah, right. Never any time. *(opens door)* She's right in here. The Big Hollywood Star is right in here! *(pushes past)*

LOUELLA:
(steps in gingerly) Who is that great huge strapping force of nature?

FRANCES:
Bill Anderson. A rising Hollywood star.

LOUELLA:
I'll give him presence but he won't be a Star.

FRANCES:
Why not?

LOUELLA:
Doesn't have "It." Now, you, my dear, are another story. I've seen all your films and seeing you in the flesh, well it's confirmed. You have "It."

FRANCES:
It?

LOUELLA:
Yes. It. I can spot "It" a mile away. And you have "It." "IT!!"

FRANCES:
Well, thank you, Miss Parsons.

LOUELLA:
Louella, please. We're going to be great friends. I only know the best people. The Stars. And you, my dear, are a rising star. You're luminous on screen. Positively luminous! And you can act?! Well, my God, no one around here can act. I thought I'd focus my piece on the Cinderella rags to riches angle—how you rose from the narrow confines of the dirt farm.

FRANCES:
My parents aren't farmers.

LOUELLA:
What a pity. It would go so well. Farmer Farmer!

FRANCES:
My father's a lawyer. And my mother's a nutritionist.

LOUELLA:
A what?

FRANCES:
She analyses food.

LOUELLA:
Oh my. *(pause)* I think it would be interesting to say you're from the Ozarks, don't you?

FRANCES:
I'm from Seattle.

LOUELLA:
That's not near the Ozarks, is it. This humble roots idea isn't exactly panning out.

FRANCES:
Maybe you should stick with the truth.

LOUELLA:
How dull. Now, my sources say-

LILLIAN enters.

LILLIAN:
Francie! I'm H-O-O-O-O-M-E!!

LOUELLA:
My! How rustic. Is this your housekeeper?

FRANCES:
My mother, Lillian Farmer. Miss Parsons.

LOUELLA:
Pleased to meet you. It's quite amazing. You two don't look at all alike.

LILLIAN:
I happen to think there's a strong family resemblance.

LOUELLA:
Sorry. I don't see it. Frances, we haven't seen you much on the Star circuit. Are you keeping your dates secret?

LILLIAN:
She doesn't have any dates. She's married.

LOUELLA:
Married?!

FRANCES:
Yes. I'm married to Bill Anderson.

LOUELLA:
To that big lug?

LILLIAN:
Wycliffe.

LOUELLA:

    Pardon?

LILLIAN:

    His name's Wycliffe.

LOUELLA:

    You don't mind if I don't mention your husband, do you,
    Miss Farmer. Husbands don't make good copy and since
    neither of you is sure what his name is, it'd be easier to
    leave him out, altogether. Now, I heard you won a beauty
    contest in Russia, is that right?

LILLIAN:

    Darn tooting! She beat those Russian broads hands down.

FRANCES:

    No—no, it wasn't a beauty contest. I was sent by the 'Voice
    of Action' newspaper—

LOUELLA:

    Isn't that a—

LILLIAN:

    No. It's not Communist.

FRANCES:

    Mamma, I think you're confusing Miss Parsons.

LOUELLA:

    It would be easier if I interviewed your daughter alone,
    Mrs. Farmer.

LILLIAN:

    My daughter is not a Communist.

LOUELLA:

    Of course not. Pleasure meeting you, Mrs. Farmer.

LILLIAN leaves.

LOUELLA:
I hope for your sake your mother is right.

FRANCES:
I'm not a Communist. However,Russia is an amazing country—

LOUELLA:
Oh God, you're not planning to tell me all about it, are you? Fans do not want to read about your visit to Russia. Hobbies? Do you have hobbies?

FRANCES:
I do charity work.

LOUELLA:
Wonderful! What sort?

FRANCES:
The Migrant Worker fund.

LOUELLA:
Any other hobbies?

FRANCES:
Our migrant workers are starving to death.

LOUELLA:
(yawns) Yes, and people are starving in China.

FRANCES:
But it's happening right here and we can do something about it.

LOUELLA:
Tell you what, next time I have dinner, I'll mail my leftovers to them. I can't put this in the article, Miss Farmer.

People know there's a depression on. We've been reading about it for years. I'd like to forget about it. That's what movies are for. There's sackcloth and ashes everywhere you look. So, if we can offer people a bit of beauty, a bit of elegance, why not? Now, what sort of film are you doing this summer. Romantic comedy? Western?

FRANCES:
Theatre.

LOUELLA:
(blankly) Theatre.

FRANCES:
Yes. I'm going to New York to play the lead in 'Golden Boy.'

LOUELLA:
(dumbfounded) You're going to be in a play?

FRANCES:
I've always wanted to pursue a stage career.

LOUELLA:
Bit ungrateful to the Studio, don't you think?

FRANCES:
What does gratitude have to do with it?

LOUELLA:
Cinderella marries the Prince and lives happily ever after. She doesn't kick him in the shins and take off for New York.

FRANCES:
If people think I'm Cinderella, they're deluded. I don't have to cater to their delusions.

LOUELLA:
Yes, you do, actually, Miss Farmer. I'm going to give you some advice. Do what you're told and don't rock the boat. You have a natural talent. Use it and enjoy it. Hollywood's a wonderful place to be. We all love being in Hollywood. *(starts to leave)* Remember that. You love being in Hollywood. *(leaves)*

LILLIAN:
(enters) My God, people are rude here. I hope she doesn't think you're a Communist.

FRANCES:
You settled her mind on that score, Mamma.

LILLIAN:
Good thing I was here. Honestly, little sister, sometimes you have no sense. Do you think you should have worn that outfit? Louella Parsons would been expecting—

FRANCES:
Mama, I have a little surprise for you. It's something you said you always wanted to do.

LILLIAN:
Really?

FRANCES:
Close your eyes.

LILLIAN:
(closes eyes)

FRANCES:
(turns around, takes out ticket from purse, hands behind back)
Okay, which hand?

LILLIAN picks one. FRANCES hands her the ticket.

53

LILLIAN:
(*studies it*) Oh—Frances.

FRANCES:
It's a trip around the world, Mamma.

LILLIAN:
Oh my!

FRANCES:
By boat.

LILLIAN:
That should take a long time.

FRANCES:
Yes. A year or so.

LILLIAN:
What a sweet thought.

FRANCES:
Well, you inspire me, Mamma.

SCENE 11

FRANCES and The Group.

FRANCES and a MALE ACTOR are rehearsing Act II, scene 3 from 'Golden Boy.' HAROLD CLURMAN directs. Other members of the Group linger in the background. ODETS enters and watches, unseen by FRANCES and the MALE ACTOR.

"*The next day: the office. LORNA and MOODY are present. She has a hangover and is restless.*"

MOODY:
"Boy, you certainly double-scotched yourself last night. What's the idea, you making a career of drinking in your old age? Headache?"

LORNA:
"No."

MOODY:
"I won't let you walk alone in the park anymore, if you do that."

LORNA:
"*(nasty in spite of her best intentions)* Well, if you stayed away from your wife for a change..."

MOODY:
"It's pretty late to bring that up, isn't it? Tuesday nights—"

LORNA:
"I can't help it—I feel like a tramp. I've felt like a tramp for years."

MOODY:
"Why do you drink like that?"

LORNA:

> "(*pointing to her chest*) Right here—there's a hard lump and I drink to dissolve it. Do you mind?"

MOODY:

> "I don't mind—as long as you keep your health."

LORNA:

> "Aw, Christ!—you and your health talks!"

MOODY:

> (*looks at CLURMAN*) Harold—

CLURMAN:

> Stop! I'm sorry. We'll have to take a break. BREAK!
> Frances, can I see you?

FRANCES:

> I'm sorry. I'm trying.

CLURMAN:

> I know. It's—ah—well—I don't know how to help you here—it's out of your range.

FRANCES:

> I know the accent's off but I'll get it.

CLURMAN:

> It's not the accent. It's being a New Yorker. It's not in your blood. You're West Coast.

FRANCES:

> Acting, Harold. Ever hear of that?

CLURMAN:

> Yeah, you're acting all right. That's all you're doing.
> Acting! (*walks away and joins the others*)

> *The Group gathers off to one side. ODETS approaches FRANCES.*

FRANCES:
Haven't seen much of you lately.

ODETS:
I know when to make myself scarce.

FRANCES:
You might as well join the chorus. They hate me.

ODETS:
It's an adjustment for everyone. You have two strikes
against you. You're an outsider and you're Hollywood.

FRANCES:
"Hollywood." What does that mean exactly?

ODETS:
That you're not a serious artist. In movies, it's all about
surface values—how you look, what you're wearing—

FRANCES:
But you can be a serious artist within the confines of your
environment.

ODETS:
If you work in an evil environment, you're bound to be
corrupted.

FRANCES:
You think Hollywood is evil?!

ODETS:
Yes. I do.

FRANCES:
Evil? I just think it's silly. There's lots of worthless fluff and
the trick is to pick through it all and make films that have
some integrity.

ODETS:

Then you're deluding yourself. The stories Hollywood
portrays are all lies. You trade away your artistic integrity
on a daily basis. Every time you do a film, a small part of
your soul is compromised. You've been bought, paid to do
someone else's bidding. It will eat away at you, a little piece
at a time. *(pause)* That, of course, is not why the people
here dislike you.

FRANCES:

Thank God for small mercies.

ODETS:

It's the Hollywood star system we despise. Its manufactured
aristocracy—

FRANCES:

It's not too late to find someone else.

ODETS:

You're going to give up?

FRANCES:

I can't get a grip on Lorna Moon. I don't know what made
you think I could be her.

ODETS:

She's in you, Frances. She's the part of you who's lost. You
have too much will. Can you even imagine what it's like to
have your fate in someone else's hands?

FRANCES:

No.

ODETS:

I want you to lose yourself. You're too much of a lady.
Swear.

FRANCES:
Swear.

ODETS:
Yes.

FRANCES:
She doesn't swear much in the play.

ODETS:
Say "Aw Christ" as though you mean it.

FRANCES:
Aw Christ. *(starts to laugh)*

ODETS:
This isn't funny.

FRANCES:
I'm sorry.

ODETS:
Let the language lead you. You'll find her as I did.

FRANCES:
Why did you bring me into all this?

ODETS:
You don't know?

FRANCES:
No. You invite me and then you disappear, leaving me to contend with people who don't like me. When they do condescend to speak to me, it's only to tell me that I'm playing Luise's part. Who's Luise?

ODETS:
Luise Rainer.

FRANCES:

Well, she's Hollywood. How did she get involved with The Group?

ODETS:

She's my—um—wife.

FRANCES:

Well, of course. You look at me like a married man. As though you'd like to devour me whole but you'd have to get permission first.

ODETS:

I haven't seen Luise for over a year. She left me.

FRANCES:

Oh. I'm sorry.

ODETS:

I'm not an easy man to be with.

FRANCES:

I'm not an easy woman.

ODETS:

What on earth possessed you to marry that big oaf?

FRANCES:

Bill?

ODETS:

Thor. Igor. Visgoth. Whatever the hell's he's calling himself now.

FRANCES:

Leif.

ODETS:

Leif?!

FRANCES:
 (laughs) Leif Erickson. He thought it had a familiar ring.

ODETS:
 (laughs)

 FRANCES and ODETS start to laugh hysterically.

FRANCES & ODETS:
 Leif Erickson! Oh God!!

ODETS:
 Frances, Frances—what a waste! What a colossal waste!
 Why? Why did you marry him?

FRANCES:
 I was in love.

ODETS:
 More damage is done in the name of love! And where is
 Prince Charming? I haven't seen him around lately.

FRANCES:
 He went back West.

ODETS:
 Don't you find it unbearably lonely, not having someone to
 talk to?

FRANCES:
 He only left yesterday.

ODETS:
 When he's here.

FRANCES:
 (bursts out laughing in spite of herself) You're mean.

ODETS:
And proud of it. You try to be good, Frances. You make sincere and determined efforts but it doesn't really suit you. You're very sexy when you're bad. *(leans in towards her)* Have dinner with me tonight.

FRANCES:
Dinner?

ODETS:
You thought I had something else in mind?

FRANCES:
(smiles) No.

ODETS:
Pick you up at eight. *(walks away)*

FRANCES:
You don't know where I live.

ODETS:
Believe me, I know exactly where you live. *(leaves)*

SCENE 12

FRANCES apartment. FRANCES and ODETS. ODETS comes from offstage.

ODETS:

You have pennants over your bed.

FRANCES:

(enters from another direction) You've been snooping.

ODETS:

(pulls out pennant from his pocket) High school pennants?

FRANCES:

Hey! Give it back! *(lunges at him to get it)*

ODETS:

(dangles it out of her reach) This isn't yours, is it?

FRANCES:

Of course not! *(reaches for it)*

ODETS:

He brings his high school pennants all the way to New York?!

FRANCES:

It makes him feel secure. I don't know! He's a boy. I married a boy! Please give it back!

ODETS:

(hands FRANCES the pennant) I don't want his pennant. I want his wife. I love you, Frances. *(kisses her passionately)*

FRANCES:

(pulls away) This isn't right.

ODETS:
> Why? Suddenly you're going to uphold middle-class
> morality. It isn't right that a beautiful intelligent woman
> should be married to a boy.

FRANCES:
> Still, he is my husband. He has no idea that I'm unhappy
> with him.

ODETS:
> He doesn't know?! Shouldn't that be grounds for divorce?
> You knew when we first met that we were destined. You
> drew me like a magnet. *(moves closer)* I am powerless to
> resist. *(kisses her passionately)*
>
> *FRANCES responds to ODET's embrace. ODETS picks her up
> and carries her off.*

SCENE 13

Opening night of "Golden Boy." FRANCES' dressing room. ODETS and HAROLD CLURMAN arrive with huge bouquets of flowers.

CLURMAN:
Well, you came through, kid. You were brilliant, Frances. I owe you an apology.

FRANCES:
It's all right, Harold. I wasn't sure I'd get it, either.

CLURMAN:
Nah, I misjudged you. I thought you were some silly Hollywood broad who thought she could buy her way in. But you were breathtaking out there tonight! Here's to you, kid.

FRANCES:
(hugs Harold)

CLURMAN:
Course Cliffie's proud of you, too, aren't you, Cliff?

ODETS:
Proud doesn't even begin to describe it. *(hugs FRANCES)* You were magnificent!

CLURMAN:
Anyway, I'm officially inviting you to join the Group.

FRANCES:
I'm here, aren't I?

CLURMAN:
On a permanent basis.

FRANCES:
Well—I—ah—have to go back at the end of the run.

HAROLD:
We're going on a year's tour. Deal came through tonight.

FRANCES:
I'd have to think it over.

HAROLD:
Think it over?! The part was written for you! There's a line-up of people down the alley and around the block, waiting for your autograph.

FRANCES:
Really?

HAROLD:
You bet. We're going for a drink so join us when you're ready. *(starts to leave)* Cliff?

ODETS:
Later. *(waits till he leaves)* What do you mean you have to go back?

FRANCES:
Let's just celebrate, all right? I don't want to talk about this now.

ODETS:
Fine, celebrate! Your public awaits! *(starts to leave)*

FRANCES:
I promised the Studio. I'll do their film, then come back here.

ODETS:
That's a bourgeois compromise of the first order. I thought you were committed. But I guess it was just empty posturing.

FRANCES:

I signed a contract.

ODETS:

So, break it! *(leaves)*

SCENE 14

FRANCES on the phone to RALPH SCHWAB.

RALPH:
You want to WHAT?!

FRANCES:
It's not such a big deal.

RALPH:
Who sez?! You sez! Reading all these snotball articles—you talking about what a bunch of yobs we are out here. Do you know what they call you here?

FRANCES:
No.

RALPH:
Highbrow! Kiss of death. "Highbrow actress Frances Farmer." Do you know what Highbrow means! No fucking parts! That's what it means!

FRANCES:
So I'll quit Hollywood and stay in New York.

RALPH:
You are under contract to do a set number of movies. You have to do them. And if you piss them off, you'll be doing some real stinkers. And I'm warning you, you're pissing them off. And those speeches about the Spanish Civil War! Would you pullease stop! Highbrow Communist actress. Double Whammy in the kiss of death department.

FRANCES:
Tell the Studio I'm taking a year off. They'll understand.
(hangs up)

RALPH:

They will not understand! Do you hear me! *(realizes that she's hung up)* Aw Christ!

SCENE 15

FRANCES and ODETS in bed.

ODETS:
   There is a radiance about you that only angels have.

FRANCES:
   I'm not being very angelic, now.

ODETS:
   Oh yes, how is Bill?

FRANCES:
   He wants a divorce.

ODETS:
   That calls for more champagne. *(brings out bottle beside bed, fills their glasses)*

ODETS:
   To damnation!

FRANCES:
   I won't drink to that.

ODETS:
   Why not? You're allowing me to ruin you.

FRANCES:
   Women don't get ruined by men, anymore.

ODETS:
   That's very modern of you but you should defend yourself.

FRANCES:
   Against what?

ODETS:
My intentions.

FRANCES:
(laughs) You're mad.

ODETS:
I'm not mad. I'm damned. Though it all adds up to the same thing. I sell my soul. The madman gives his away. And the body does what it pleases. You should refuse me, Frances. *(pause)* Do you believe in God?

FRANCES:
I gave Him up for dead a long time ago.

ODETS:
He disappointed you, did He?

FRANCES:
No. In fact, He gave me everything I wanted.

ODETS:
Maybe He still does. You seem to have led a charmed life. Whom do you owe? Or did you cast your lot in with the Devil?

FRANCES:
I don't owe anything to anyone.

ODETS:
(strokes her) The moment I laid eyes on you, I wanted you and here you are in my bed. I always get what I want, but unlike you, I know whom I owe. And then I get bored and I want something else. And you will have lost your power of refusal. But it is not my problem. You are my desire, not my problem. Anyway, you are madly in love with me, so there's not much you can do when your body is urging you to fuck. There's not much you can do. Except refuse.

FRANCES:
   (starts to get out of bed) All right, then. I refuse. You are a
   bloody lunatic.

ODETS:
   (takes her arm) I don't love you anymore, Frances.

FRANCES:
   I don't care.

ODETS:
   Don't lie. You care very much.

FRANCES:
   No. I don't.

ODETS:
   You really are becoming like Lorna Moon. It's amazing
   how one's creations come to life.

FRANCES:
   (putting on her clothes in a fury) I am not one of your fucking
   creations! And I don't love you. I fuck you because I feel
   like it. It has nothing to do with my soul, power of refusal,
   being mad or being damned. I fuck you because I feel like
   fucking you and when I don't, I will stop. And that's all
   there fucking well is to it!

ODETS:
   Tough talk, but I'm not buying it.

   "O Rose, thou art sick
   The invisible worm
   that flies in the night..."

FRANCES:
   SHUT UP!

ODETS:

"...in the howling storm.
Has found out thy bed
of crimson joy..."

FRANCES:

STOP IT! DO YOU HEAR ME!

ODETS:

"...And his dark secret love
Does thy life destroy."

FRANCES:

STOP IT!!

(pause)

FRANCES:

Why are you doing this to me?

ODETS:

Because you want it. You want to be ruined. Oh sorry, I
forgot your distaste for the Victorian. You want to be
fucked. All the Christian martyrs wanted to be fucked.
Saint Theresa, Saint—

FRANCES:

You're insane.

ODETS:

Saint Dymphna.

FRANCES:

What?

ODETS:

Patron saint for the insane. I know my saints and martyrs.
Saint Frances. *(laughs)* That's what you want to be. Poor
old Saint Frances silly cunt.

FRANCES:
SHUT UP AND LEAVE ME ALONE!!

A woman walks in. It is LUISE RAINER, Clifford Odets' wife.

LUISE:
My my, what a racket!

ODETS:
Darling, you're back. *(hurriedly puts his clothes on)*

LUISE:
Yes. I told you I was coming.

ODETS:
I must have got the dates mixed up.

LUISE:
Apparently.

FRANCES:
(to LUISE) Who the fuck are you?

LUISE:
Mrs. Fucking Odets, that's who!

ODETS:
Darling, this is Frances Farmer.

LUISE:
Oh. Yes, of course. You took over for me while I was away. I hear you were very good.

ODETS:
(laughs nervously)

LUISE:
Going back to Hollywood. Your loss, my gain. *(takes the champagne)* How sweet, a going-away present. Well thank you very much, dear. Even if you have drunk most of it.

FRANCES:

(grabs bottle back) I am not leaving!

LUISE:

Well, Cliffie and I have to go out.

FRANCES:

I am playing Lorna Moon on the tour.

LUISE:

(to ODETS) Darling, were you up to your usual tricks?

ODETS:

You weren't coming back. We needed someone in the
interim.

FRANCES:

SOMEONE IN THE INTERIM??! I LIVED HERE, GOD-
DAMMIT! *(to LUISE)* WE MADE LOVE IN YOUR BED!!

LUISE:

Yes. I can see that. He does that all the time.

> *FRANCES lunges at LUISE.*

LUISE:

(leaps back) Aaaaagh! Cliffie!!

> *ODETS grabs FRANCES. They engage in a struggle,*
> *FRANCES trying to hit ODETS with the bottle of champagne,*
> *ODETS dodging the attempts. LUISE stands off to one side*
> *and watches.*

FRANCES:

(sobbing) You said you loved me!

LUISE:

There's only one person Cliffie loves and we're both
looking at him.

ODETS:

> *(to FRANCES)* Your money and your talent were very useful to us.

FRANCES:

> *(disbelieving)* What?

ODETS:

> Whatever I felt for you, it's over. It's time for you to go home. *(tries to push FRANCES out the door)*

FRANCES:

> You goddamn hypocrite!

ODETS:

> It's the truth.

> *FRANCES suddenly gives up the struggle and goes to the door.*

FRANCES:

> YOU LYING, THIEVING HYPOCRITE!! *(exits)*

SCENE 16

FRANCES' home in Hollywood. FRANCES arrives home with two enormous suitcases. A woman (GLORIA GARNET) is there. Her hair is bleached blonde. She is dressed in sleazy lounge clothes of the 30's.

FRANCES:
> *(enters, stares at GLORIA)*

GLORIA:
> Well, it's about time! You wouldn't believe the mess this place was in. You can start with the windows.

FRANCES:
> Who are you?

GLORIA:
> Gloria Garnet. Here. *(whips out a pen and paper- signs her autograph—stuffs it in FRANCES' coat)* In three years time, that'll be worth som'thn'. *(looks at suitcases)* You got your stuff with you. Dis isn't a live-in job, ya know.

FRANCES:
> Why are you in my house? *(looks around)* The walls are yellow.

GLORIA:
> I live here.

FRANCES:
> *(smiles)* No. *(smiles again)* No. This is my house.

GLORIA:
> Oh great—wait goddamn forever and get a goddamn fruitcake. Can't get decent help anywhere.

FRANCES:
> I AM NOT THE HELP. I LIVE HERE.

GLORIA:
Don't get tough with me, sister, or I'll call the police.

FRANCES:
(looks around) Where's my furniture! Why are the walls yellow!

GLORIA:
(tries to guide her out) Come on, sister. Maybe, you live next door. Maybe you live in the next county.

FRANCES:
(struggles) This is my house!

> *They struggle.*

GLORIA:
GET OUT!!

FRANCES:
BUT I LIVE HERE!! I HAVE A KEY!!

GLORIA:
(stops) Aw, hold your horses. You're that pushy broad the Studios are mad at.

FRANCES:
What?

GLORIA:
They told me you'd probably show up but like, that was a while ago, so I forgot. What's your name?

FRANCES:
Frances Farmer.

GLORIA:
That's right. The Commie. Some government people were here, too. They packed up all your stuff and moved it to the Knickerbocker Hotel. Ain't life a bitch.

FRANCES:
 (starts to reel around) I—have—to—sit—down.

GLORIA:
 (pulls her a chair) Do you want a trank?

FRANCES:
 (sits, nods)

GLORIA:
 (goes out, returns with a glass of water and pills)

FRANCES:
 (takes one)

GLORIA:
 Look, I feel real bad. Got your house. Got your parts.

FRANCES:
 (looks up) Got my parts?

GLORIA:
 Well, yeah, some of them. Actually, not the ones I wanted.
 Lana got the ones I really wanted.

FRANCES:
 Oh. So, they've given my movies away. So then, I'm out.
 I've been fired. I'm fre-e-e-eeee!

GLORIA:
 Nah. You're still in. You just got lousy movies.

FRANCES:
 Oh.

GLORIA:
 Lunch time. *(takes a pill)*

FRANCES:
Bennie?

GLORIA:
Keeps the flab off. *(looks at FRANCES)* Did you know that the camera adds—

FRANCES:
Fifteen pounds. Yes. I know that.

GLORIA:
No offense, but you could stand to lose a few.

FRANCES:
Sure, why not. *(takes a Bennie)* Why the hell not!

SCENE 17

FRANCES and RALPH SCHWAB. FRANCES bursts in. She looks very dishevelled.

FRANCES:
WHAT THE HELL HAPPENED TO MY HOUSE?!

RALPH:
Christ! You look awful! Where have you been!

FRANCES:
I've been to my house! And it's not mine anymore, you bastard!

RALPH:
Blame the Bank. You were behind in your payments. I couldn't find you to tell you.

FRANCES:
I left you the cheques.

RALPH:
They bounced. No money. All gone.

FRANCES:
What?

RALPH:
You've been very charitable lately. Group Theatre's Civil War fund. Remember?

FRANCES:
(looks blank)

RALPH:
Where have you been for the last month?

FRANCES:

I went for a long drive. *(takes a pill)* Gained weight.

RALPH:

Watch those things.

FRANCES:

I have to get down to my fighting form. Get back on the silver screen.

RALPH:

Look, the Studio's stuck you with some real dogs. They're making you do penance. Your first gig's in Mexico.

FRANCES:

Do you think it's far enough out of town?

RALPH:

I sure as hell hope so.

SCENE 18

FRANCES, drunk, alone on stage.

FRANCES:
I am exploring my nether regions. I have become a slattern, a trull, a whore. My words are foul and my thoughts fetid. *(takes a swig of whiskey)* They put me in bad movies and that is what I give them. B-A-A-A-D. Smelly, dirty, filthy, B-A-A-A-D. I am a pig wallowing in my own manure. *(smiles)* It feels good.

SCENE 19

LOUELLA PARSONS and FRANCES FARMER.

LOUELLA:
(composes) Cinderella goes back to the ashes on a liquor-slicked highway. *(nods to herself)* Yes, perfect.

FRANCES:
(bursts in, looking extremely dishevelled) (waves a paper at Miss Parsons) How dare you print these lies about me!

LOUELLA:
You're not looking well, darling. Hangover from last night?

FRANCES:
I am not a drunk and I did not have a nervous breakdown in Mexico.

LOUELLA:
You did assault the director.

FRANCES:
No. I did not. But I wish I had. He could have used a punch in the face.

LOUELLA:
Can I quote you on that? And really darling, how did you manage it? No one gets deported from Mexico.

FRANCES:
I WAS NOT DEPORTED! I got sick.

LOUELLA:
Too much tequila?

FRANCES:
Traveller's flu. And they took me to the nearest—

LOUELLA:
Sanitarium.

FRANCES:
Hospital.

LOUELLA:
Across the border?

FRANCES:
Yes, but—

LOUELLA:
Accompanied by the Mexican police.

FRANCES:
I WAS NOT DEPORTED!

LOUELLA:
Please don't make a scene, Miss Farmer. I'd save that for
your movies. Such as they are.

FRANCES:
Why are you trying to ruin my career? Who's paying you to
do it? The government?

LOUELLA:
Don't get paranoid, dear. I simply report on events. You're
the one creating the news.

FRANCES:
But you're writing lies about me!

LOUELLA:
I write a gossip column. And I'm sorry, darling, but if you
go around telling people to go "F" themselves, it's not
going to be nice gossip. You really should take my advice.
Three simple things: comb your hair, wash your face and
keep your mouth shut and maybe, you might salvage what
remains of your career.

FRANCES:

I don't care if you approve of me. Or even like me. All I ask is that you print the truth.

LOUELLA:

You've got your priorities wrong, darling. You should care very much what I think of you. You should want me to like you. Because the truth is entirely dependent on who's telling it. And right now, I'm telling it. And if I say you're having a nervous breakdown, darling, you're having a nervous breakdown.

FRANCES:

What do you want from me?

LOUELLA:

A little respect.

FRANCES:

GO FUCK YOURSELF! *(leaves)*

SCENE 20

FRANCES FARMER and EDNA BURGE.

FRANCES:
>   *(rushes in)*

EDNA:
>   Late again, Miss Farmer?

FRANCES:
>   It appears that way, doesn't it. *(sits down)*

EDNA:
>   *(starts to arrange hair)* I'm sorry for all the trouble you've
>   been having.

FRANCES:
>   Mmmm. *(pause)* OW!

EDNA:
>   Sorry. Little snarl, here. You know, you were such a pretty
>   sweet-natured girl when you first come here. I remember
>   thinking that girl's going to go far. And I look at you now,
>   your hair's in a mess and your career's going down the
>   tubes.

FRANCES:
>   Do you mind?

EDNA:
>   Don't take offense. It's cause I like you that I'm even
>   bringing it up. Drink and high living. Does it every time.

FRANCES:
>   Would you please shut up and do my hair.

EDNA:

I'm just trying to help. Offer a bit of advice. *(pause) (she arranges hair)* I may just be a hairdresser but I know a helluva lot about this business. Diet pills. They're the problem. Makes all the youngsters cranky and bad-tempered. But drink's the worst. Sometimes, I ask myself: Edna, why are you here working for these people? Most of them are no better than you but they treat you like dirt. They think they're bloody princesses. Of course, the Studio encourages that sort of thing. Stars. Unknown sluts with looks and a figure and they become stars. Now, if I had looks and a figure, I could have been a star, too. But you can't get too far on piano legs and a harelip. It's been operated on, but it still shows—

FRANCES:

If you don't shut up by the time I count to ten, I'm going to punch you in the face.

EDNA:

I used to like you, Miss Farmer. I used to think you were different from all the rest.

FRANCES:

One—Two—Three—

EDNA:

And you should stay off the booze. That's what I'm trying to tell you. Booze is the worst thing for—

FRANCES:

I was not drunk—damn it. FOUR—FIVE—

EDNA:

Well, you must be on something. Cause you're not nice, anymore. You used to be nice.

FRANCES:
Listen, you stupid old cow, if I don't feel like being "nice" that's just too fucking bad. It's your job to comb my hair so COMB MY HAIR. SIX—SEVEN—EIGHT—

EDNA:
No. *(crosses arms)* Not until you apologize.

FRANCES:
Apologize?! All right, I'll do it myself. *(tries to grab comb)*

EDNA:
NO! Let go of that!!

> *They struggle.*

FRANCES:
(gets comb) (starts to arrange hair)

EDNA:
You're a drunken slut! That's what you are!

FRANCES:
(wheels around) TEN! *(slaps EDNA in the face)*

(storms out the door)

EDNA:
(falls back, clutching jaw)

SCENE 21

FRANCES in bed. (loud knocking)

POLICEMAN:
Open up! Police! You're under arrest.

FRANCES:
Huh? What time it is?

POLICE:
(knocks loudly) Police! Open up!

FRANCES:
Why?

The door bursts open. Two POLICEMEN barge in.

FRANCES:
Get out of here!

POLICE 1:
Miss Farmer.

FRANCES:
Get out of my room!

POLICE 1:
You're under arrest, Miss Farmer. Charges for assault from Miss Edna Burge—

FRANCES:
I don't know any Edna Burge.

POLICE 2:
You dislocated her jaw.

FRANCES:
I don't know what you're talking about. Get out of here!

POLICE 1:
We have orders to arrest you.

FRANCES:
All right. You stay here and I'll get out. *(runs out the door)*

The POLICEMEN run after her and grab her.

FRANCES:
Jesus Christ, let go of me!! You can't come barging into my room in the middle of the night.

POLICE 1:
Yes, we can, Miss Farmer.

FRANCES:
I've got to call my lawyer. I believe that is one of my civil rights.

POLICE 1:
Come along! *(yanks her away)*

FRANCES:
(struggling) I have my civil rights, goddammit!

POLICE 1:
(heads FRANCES out the door)

POLICE 2:
She doesn't have any clothes on.

POLICE 1:
Bring them along. Maybe she'll change her mind in the car.

FRANCES:
Godammit! Go to Hell! Get your hands offa me! You cock-sucker!! You can't do this to me—you goddamn pigs!!

They stuff a sock in her mouth and take her away.

SCENE 22

FRANCES, in jail.

FRANCES:

Justice is swift when it chooses to be. Why did I punch that
woman in the face? She was incredibly annoying and sometimes you just have to let people know what you think of
them. A mad doctor came to my cell today and asked me if
I was hearing voices. I said, "Yes" meaning his. And the
moron nods and mumbles "paranoid schizophrenic." So I
said, "Listen asshole, it's your voice I"m hearing." And he
said, "Are you hearing my voice, now?" "Of course not,
prickhead, you're not talking now but I heard your voice a
few seconds ago." And he said when? And suddenly I was
in this Abbott and Costello routine arguing over who's on
first. So the dickhead talks to my mother, persuades her
I'm crazy. I'm bankrupt, ergo I must be crazy. And they're
sending me to La Crescenta sanitarium. I like jail. It's
brutal and organized. Everything is very clear here. I don't
want to play pingpong with a bunch of neurotic actors. I
want to stay in jail!

SCENE 23

Sanitarium. DR. SWAN and FRANCES FARMER.

SWAN:
You wanted to see me, Miss Farmer.

FRANCES:
Yes, Doctor, I'm sure it's been an oversight but I just wanted to remind you that my term sentence is up and I'm ready to leave.

SWAN:
I'll be the judge of that, Miss Farmer.

FRANCES:
You can't keep me here! My time's up.

SWAN:
You're still a bit tense, Miss Farmer.

FRANCES:
That's because I got railroaded into this joint. I served my sentence and now I want OUT!

SWAN:
You're definitely tense.

FRANCES:
Could I use your phone, please. *(goes to phone)*

SWAN:
(stops her) You have become very hostile in the last few weeks. I have recommended a special insulin treatment to isolate your tensions.

A NURSE arrives with a needle.

93

FRANCES:
Get that stuff away from me! Get away from me!!

*DR. SWAN and the NURSE grab FRANCES, hold her down
and inject the needle into her arm. FRANCES goes into
convulsions, screams in a panting fashion—then passes
out—body still trembling.*

SCENE 24

FRANCES and DR. SWAN.

FRANCES:

Please—I beg you. Don't do this to me. It's destroying my mind. I can't think. I can't concentrate. I can't do anything, anymore. I'm losing it.

SWAN:

It?

FRANCES:

My drive. My creativity.

SWAN:

Why do you object so strenuously to insulin therapy? You were committing far greater damage to your body before. You see, your addiction to Benzedrine—

FRANCES:

If I want to take bennies and be an alcoholic, then that's my concern.

SWAN:

It is until you start assaulting people. Then, it's our concern. I've put you on a ninety day intensive programme.

FRANCES:

Please let me call home!

SWAN:

It's best that you don't contact your parents, now. The isolation is doing you a world of good.

FRANCES:

Please!

SWAN:

> *(smiles)* I've seen all your movies, Miss Farmer.

FRANCES:

> You cocksucker!

SWAN:

> Such language! It would be easier if you'd simply co-operate.

> > *DR. SWAN leaves. A NURSE enters. FRANCES goes into a defense posture, prepared to be injected.*

NURSE:

> Walkies? *(holds out a white coat)*

FRANCES:

> What? *(pause)* Sure, why not? *(reaches down and pulls out an enormous book)*

NURSE:

> You can't walk and read.

FRANCES:

> No, but I find a book very comforting, just the same. *(clutches onto book)*

> > *The NURSE gives up. They walk for a while.*

FRANCES:

> Can we walk over here, Nurse? The flowers are so beautiful by the wall. *(walks away from NURSE)*

NURSE:

> *(quickly joins FRANCES, glances at book)* 'War and Peace.' Geez! It's big. How do you get through all that?

FRANCES:

> I'm having a lot of difficulty with it, now. I didn't before I came in here.

NURSE:

Now now, I'm sure you're just imagining these lapses. We think you're much better. Isn't this a Russian book? Are you sure you're allowed to read this? It's not subversive, is it?

FRANCES:

Of course not. It's before the Revolution.

NURSE:

Huh?

FRANCES:

Forget it.

They approach the wall.

FRANCES:

Oh! Look at that rose! Isn't it beautiful! *(bends down to sniff rose)*

NURSE:

Yeah—it's nice.

FRANCES:

(smells it) Oh, smell it. It has a lovely scent.

NURSE:

(bends down to sniff rose) Yeah, it's all right.

FRANCES:

(bonks NURSE over the head with the book)

NURSE:

(slumps down) Ooooooh.

FRANCES climbs over the wall.

SCENE 25

FRANCES and LILLIAN.

LILLIAN:

(holding letter) The nerve! They're still demanding that you finish the treatments.

FRANCES:

It's a lucky thing I got out of there alive. How could you let them do that to me!

LILLIAN:

How was I to know! They said it was harmless and it would snap you out it.

FRANCES:

Snap me out of what?

LILLIAN:

Dr. Swan said the pills combined with your heavy drinking—well, you've inherited that nasty little problem from your father. I've been dealing with him for years.

FRANCES:

Yeah and look at him.

LILLIAN:

Are you implying that it's my fault.

FRANCES:

Of course not, Mamma. I'm sorry. I don't know what I'm saying. My mind feels like it's been scattered out like a jigsaw puzzle.

LILLIAN:

It's all the fault of that Group. They made you a Communist. They made you give all your money away.

FRANCES:
Mamma, I am not a Communist.

LILLIAN:
You don't need to hide it from me, dear. Men from the government came and told your father and me all about it.

FRANCES:
And I guess they suggested that I go to the "rest" home.

LILLIAN:
They're trying to help you, dear. You've been indoctrinated by the Communists.

FRANCES:
The only people who've done anything to my brain are our wonderful doctors in the U.S. of A. And they've really hammered away at it.

LILLIAN:
We'll put all this behind us. When you're back at work, you'll feel much better. Your agent called and he says the Studio feels so bad about your hard times that they're actually offering you decent parts. Isn't that great! Now, you haven't made the A list yet but—

FRANCES:
Mamma, I don't know how to explain this. I don't feel I'm myself, anymore.

LILLIAN:
Well, I've been telling you that.

FRANCES:
No. It's not Communism. It's not the Group. It's something to do with making movies.

LILLIAN:
What?

FRANCES:

Each time I do a film, something gets taken out of me. My strength is robbed. Especially when I do a bad film. Then it's as though all that dross enters into me and fills me up.

LILLIAN:

What on earth are you talking about?

FRANCES:

I'm not going back to Hollywood, Mamma.

LILLIAN:

You're going to turn down a million dollar career— something you've been dreaming about for years—

FRANCES:

Something you've been dreaming about. Not me!

LILLIAN:

Look, I wasn't born with a beautiful face or a beautiful body but I got as far as I could with what I've got. And I've made sure you got as far as you could—

FRANCES:

It wasn't all your doing, Mamma.

LILLIAN:

But I go away on that stupid cruise. Leave you on your own and you ruin everything! But, I'll get it back. I'll make sure we get it back.

FRANCES:

BUT I DON'T WANT IT!

LILLIAN:

You owe me, little sister.

FRANCES:

> I don't owe you anything! And I'm not your little sister!
> I'm not your little girl! I'm not your little anything! Do you
> understand!!

LILLIAN:

> What's wrong with you. What ever happened to my sweet
> little—

FRANCES:

> Christ! Everything you say is a broken record. You got
> stuck on one track and you just keep going round. You're
> going senile, Mamma.

LILLIAN:

> Senile?! You're crazy! Who are you to tell me I'm senile!

FRANCES:

> I'm your daughter, Mamma. Two sides of the same fucking
> coin.

LILLIAN:

> Stop swearing! Stop it! There'll be no swearing in this
> house!!

FRANCES:

> How do you fucking plan to stop me, Mamma. *(grabs her)*
> You're fucking senile. You're a fucking senile old woman!!

LILLIAN:

> *(shrieks)* Aaagh! Let go of me!!

FRANCES:

> *(lets go) (walks away)*

LILLIAN:

> You've gone mad! Where're you going? I forbid you to
> leave this house!!

FRANCES:

I'm going out to get drunk! Roaring stinking drunk!
(slams door)

SCENE 26

The next day. Breakfast.

LILLIAN:
> *(looking out the window)*

FRANCES:
> *(enters)* Morning, Mamma.

LILLIAN:
> *(no response)*

FRANCES:
> Look, I'm sorry about yesterday. *(pause)* What's out there, anyway?

LILLIAN:
> Oh nothing.

FRANCES:
> If it's nothing, why are you looking at it?

LILLIAN:
> Have some juice. *(she does not turn around)*

FRANCES:
> Mamma, what's going on?

LILLIAN:
> *(still looking out the window)* The boys are here.

FRANCES:
> What boys?

The door bursts open. Hospital ATTENDANTS rush in.

ATTENDANT 1:
> Is this the patient?

LILLIAN:
Yes.

ATTENDANT 1:
   (grabs FRANCES, starts to drag her off)

FRANCES:
   Mamma! What's going on?! Let go of me!!

ATTENDANT 2:
   (hands LILLIAN an invoice) Sign here, please.

LILLIAN:
   (signs)

FRANCES:
   What the hell is going on!! MAMMA!! HELP ME!!

LILLIAN:
   It's for your own good, little sister.

ATTENDANT 1:
   (grabbing FRANCES) You take an end, Harry.

FRANCES:
   (struggles) Help! Help!! MAMMA!! MAMMA!!!

   The ATTENDANTS drag FRANCES away, kicking and screaming. LILLIAN sits down and stares out blankly.

SCENE 27

*FRANCES is brought in before a panel of three people:
DR. NICHOLSON, DR. BETELGEUSE* who is wearing a
polka-dot bowtie and JUDGE FRATER.*

** "Betelgeuse" is pronounced as "Bettellgehrseh," not
"Beeteljuice." This does not necessarily mean the Doctor is
German.*

FRANCES:
(*sees FRATER*) Judge Frater. Oh Christ, so you're behind all
this!

FRATER:
I've said for years she was dangerous.

NICHOLSON:
We're here to examine you, Mrs. Anderson. Your—

FRANCES:
My name is Frances Farmer.

NICHOLSON:
The records say Mrs. Anderson. Your married name, I
believe.

FRANCES:
I'm not married anymore so my name is Frances Farmer.

NICHOLSON:
Not here, I'm afraid. Here, you are Mrs. Anderson. Now,
your attorney, Mr. Stone, has advised that you be brought
before us for assessment.

FRANCES:
Who's Mr. Stone? Assessed for what?

NICHOLSON:

Your sanity. Your mother has sworn out a public complaint
against you.

FRANCES:

What?! My mother's gone berserk. Anyway, if it's a public
complaint, what am I doing here? Why aren't I being tried
in a court?

FRATER:

Mr. Stone has waived your right to a jury trial.

FRANCES:

What! Did you arrange that! You son of a bitch!

NICHOLSON:

Really, Mrs. Anderson, your language—

FRANCES:

My language! You can take my language and shove it up
your fucking ass! I demand to see a lawyer.

NICHOLSON:

You've seen your lawyer.

FRANCES:

I've never laid eyes on the motherfucker.

NICHOLSON:

You're being very belligerent, Mrs. Anderson.

BETELGEUSE:

Are you a Communist?

FRANCES:

Are you my lawyer? (to NICHOLSON) Is that motherfucker
Stone?

NICHOLSON:
Of course not. That is Dr. Betelgeuse. He is here to assess
you.

BETELGEUSE:
Pleased to meet you.

FRANCES:
Eat shit.

BETELGEUSE:
Well really!

NICHOLSON:
Now, your mother states that you have rejected your
profession and only means of livelihood. Is that true?

FRANCES:
Yes. I felt in the long run, whoring was not an honourable
profession.

FRATER:
You were an actress, I believe, Mrs. Anderson.

FRANCES:
I was a whore.

BETELGEUSE:
 (jots note)

FRANCES:
Hey Polka-Dot. Whatcha doing?

BETELGEUSE:
Is she referring to me?

NICHOLSON:
I believe so.

BETELGEUSE:
Why is she calling me Polka-Dot?

NICHOLSON:
I think she means your tie.

BETELGEUSE:
Is there something wrong with my tie?

NICHOLSON:
Your mother said you were prone to attacks of violence,
some on her, personally.

FRANCES:
Have you met my mother?

NICHOLSON:
Yes, of course.

FRANCES:
Try living with her for a few weeks and see if that doesn't
drive you to acts of violence.

NICHOLSON:
Your mother is not on trial here.

FRANCES:
You're taking her word against mine, aren't you?

NICHOLSON:
Your mother does not have a record of commitment. You,
however, do.

FRANCES:
My mother is a seventy-year-old crone who's gone senile.
She imagines things.

NICHOLSON:
She didn't imagine the bruises on her arm when you
attacked her.

FRANCES:
I did not attack her.

NICHOLSON:
Where did the bruises come from?

FRANCES:
A man gets in a fight and punches someone in the face.
Does that mean he's insane? You want to find me guilty.
The question is why.

BETELGEUSE:
Ah. Paranoid schizophrenic.

FRANCES:
Oh shut up, Polka-Dot. You people have already decided
that I'm insane.

NICHOLSON:
You are imagining plots.

FRANCES:
I'm not imagining this trial. This fucking kangaroo court.

BETELGEUSE:
Are you a Communist?

FRANCES:
Are you an asshole?

NICHOLSON:
Answer the question, please, Mrs. Anderson.

FRANCES:
No. I am not a Communist.

NICHOLSON:
Your mother says you have many friends who are
Communists and that you have squandered all your money
on left-wing causes.

FRANCES:
I see. And that is the real reason you're locking me up, isn't it? I've been deluded. I thought I lived in a free country. *(sings)* "America, America..."*(continues to sing when NICHOLSON talks to her)*

NICHOLSON:
Please don't sing, Mrs. Anderson.

FRANCES:
But I'm singing about this wonderful country I live in. "Land of the brave and the free." *(sings some more)*

NICHOLSON:
You're a very sick woman, Mrs. Anderson.

FRANCES:
"O Rose, thou art sick,
The invisible worm..."

BETELGEUSE:
She's mad.

FRANCES:
"That flies in the night
in the howling storm..."

NICHOLSON:
This isn't getting us anywhere.

FRANCES:
"Has found out thy bed
of crimson joy..."

NICHOLSON:
Enough poetry, Mrs. Anderson. The assessment's over.

FRANCES:
"And his dark secret love
Does thy life destroy."

NICHOLSON:

> *(stands up and reads out)* "I have heard the testimony of the witnesses..."

FRANCES:

> Witnesses? What witnesses?!

NICHOLSON:

> "And personally examined Mrs. F.E. Anderson and I find that said person is insane."

FRANCES:

> Insane?! I haven't had a trial!!

FRATER:

> *(to FRANCES)* Through the power vested in me by the sovereign state of Washington, I hereby order you to immediate confinement to the Western Washington State Hospital for the Insane at Steilacoom.

> *The DOCTORS lead her out of the room.*

FRANCES:

> I'll find a lawyer. I'll find someone. You can't do this to me!

NICHOLSON:

> We're doing nothing to you, Mrs. Anderson. You're doing it to yourself.

FRANCES:

> *(struggling)* YOU CAN'T DO THIS TO ME!! I'M A FREE PERSON!! THIS IS A FREE COUNTRY!!!

END OF ACT ONE

111

Act Two

SCENE 1

*Steilacoom. Ward. MISS CARLYLE lies in a cot. FRANCES
is in front of the stage. She addresses the audience.*

FRANCES:
Lives of quiet desperation is not simply a handy phrase
one uses to impress people. It is the truth. We are all
quietly desperate. Everyone—save for the crazies. They are
noisily desperate and that is why they are here. Nobody
likes a fuss. People will tolerate fusses from babies and
children, but nobody likes it. And when you're over thirty
and you make a fuss, you better watch out because you'll
find yourself being severely edited. Then censored. And
finally, if you're very noisy and very fussy, locked up.

(goes and sits back in her cot)

NURSE:
(enters) Good morning, Miss Farmer. Time for shock.

FRANCES:
Please. Call me Mrs. Anderson. I'm tired of signing
autographs.

NURSE:
But everyone here knows who you are.

FRANCES:
Really. Is that so? *(points to grogged-out patient)* Do you think
she knows?

NURSE:
Well—ah—

FRANCES:
>   (*pokes her*) Hey! Wake up! Who am I?

PATIENT:
>   (*wakes up*) (*looks at FRANCES*)

FRANCES:
>   Who am I?

CARLYLE:
>   You're a faceless sinner.

FRANCES:
>   Yeah—but what's my name?

CARLYLE:
>   Faceless sinners don't have names.

NURSE:
>   All right, Miss Farmer, you've proved your point. Now, don't pester the other patients.

FRANCES:
>   Pester?! You have no idea what goes on here, do you? She was raped last night.

NURSE:
>   Yes. I'm sure.

FRANCES:
>   By one of the orderlies.

NURSE:
>   Yes yes, that's all very well. Now, let's prepare for shock.

FRANCES:
>   You don't believe me.

NURSE:

    Of course I don't believe you. You're insane. Now, come along. *(pulls her)*

FRANCES:

    (resists)

NURSE:

    You're just making it harder for yourself. We'll just have to restrain you.

FRANCES:

    Get your fucking hands off me!

CARLYLE:

    I'll go. I like shock. Let me go.

NURSE:

    Now, Miss Carlyle, you don't need shock.

CARLYLE:

    I'll go. I'm ready.

FRANCES:

    She's nuts.

CARLYLE:

    Please please, let me have shock. I like shock.

NURSE:

    You can't have shock!

CARLYLE:

    But I want shock!

NURSE:

    Well, you can't have it!

CARLYLE:

> *(sniffles)* All right. If you say I can't have shock, I won't have shock. Because you know best. I'm getting better. I'm going to be all better, aren't I?

NURSE:

> Yes, Miss Carlyle, you're making rapid progress.

CARLYLE:

> Goody goody.

FRANCES:

> I think I'm going to be sick.

NURSE:

> *(leads FRANCES away)* Come along, Miss Farmer.

FRANCES:

> That is truly nauseating.

CARLYLE:

> *(smiles)*

SCENE 2

LILLIAN FARMER, alone on stage.

LILLIAN:

Sometimes, I answer her fan mail. I pretend I'm her and I
spend the whole morning writing replies. It's like Francie
and I are the same person. I'm not big and fat and ugly.
I'm young and beautiful and I have wavy blonde hair and
large blue eyes. Why was I born with this body? It's not the
way I feel. Francie is the way I feel. She and I are soul
sisters. When I look in the mirror, I see Francie's face.
Except, every so often, when I dress up to go out and I put
on my black and white suit and my black and white shoes
and my hat with the feather and I go down the stairs—
feeling like an elegant woman—and out of the corner of
my eye—in the mirror, I catch sight of this big old crone
wearing a silly hat. And I realize that's me. I'm never going
to look like Francie. Never. But I can always pretend.
There's nothing wrong with pretending, is there?

SCENE 3

Steilacoom. Hydrotherapy. FRANCES FARMER and MISS CARLYLE are in tubs of cold water. FRANCES is boxed in up to her neck. MISS CARLYLE sits freely in a tub. She has a yellow duck which she plays with.

CARLYLE:

(*singing*) "Rubber Ducky, you're the one
You make bathtime so much fun
Rubber Ducky—I'm awfully fond of—
Rubber Ducky—I'm awfully fond of—
You! You! BooBoo Bee Doo
QUACK QUACK QUACK!"

FRANCES:

Christ! Would you shut up!

CARLYLE:

I'm not Christ.

FRANCES:

I didn't say you were.

CARLYLE:

Yes, you did.

FRANCES:

Forget it.

CARLYLE:

All right. (*sings*)
"When I sit alone in my t-u-u-u-u-bby. I gotta rubber ducky who's cute and yellow and chu-u-u-u-bby!"

FRANCES:

Shut up!! What the fuck have you got to be so fucking cheerful about?!

CARLYLE:
   I killed my husband.

FRANCES:
   (stares at her)

CARLYLE:
   I like hydro.

FRANCES:
   You fucking like everything. You fucking like being raped.

CARLYLE:
   You shouldn't swear.

FRANCES:
   Why the fuck not.

CARLYLE:
   You'll have to stay in longer if you swear.

FRANCES:
   Do you like being slammed in icy cold water and left to rot?

CARLYLE:
   I don't mind it.

FRANCES:
   Why not?

CARLYLE:
   It's a small price to pay for peace of mind. *(sings)* "Rubber Ducky, you're the one..."

FRANCES:
   Oh—shut the fuck up!!

CARLYLE:

You'll never get out of here, you know.

FRANCES:

What are you, a prophet?

CARLYLE:

No. An angel of light. You catch more flies with honey than with vinegar. *(laughs)* I'll get out of here long before you.

FRANCES:

How do you plan to do that? Fly?

CARLYLE:

Can't tell you.

FRANCES:

Why not?

CARLYLE:

Cause if I tell you, you'll get out before you've learned the lesson. And then, they'll send you to Hell.

FRANCES:

If being stuck in an ice bath for five hours isn't your idea of Hell, I'd hate to know what is.

CARLYLE:

This isn't Hell. Ward D. That's Hell.

FRANCES:

Look, if I ever get out of here—I sure as hell won't be coming back.

CARLYLE:

It's a pity you can't act. *(laughs)*

FRANCES:

At least I'm not crazy.

CARLYLE:

I wouldn't tell people that if I were you. Sounds as though you think you're better than them.

FRANCES:

I didn't murder my husband.

CARLYLE:

It doesn't make you better than me. We're all equal in the sight of God.

FRANCES:

God is dead.

CARLYLE:

You deny Him but I know you believe.

FRANCES:

I believe in free will.

CARLYLE:

You put yourself in here?!

FRANCES:

No, of course not.

CARLYLE:

Someone with a stronger will put you in here?

FRANCES:

My mother put me in here but that's not—

CARLYLE:

So you believe in your mother instead of God?

FRANCES:
What?

CARLYLE:
You don't deny she exists.

FRANCES:
I hate her guts.

CARLYLE:
Like God.

FRANCES:
Pardon?

CARLYLE:
He exists. You just don't like Him. You say you don't believe in Him but really, you just don't like Him.

FRANCES:
So what you're saying is that I'm at war with God?

CARLYLE:
I'm not saying anything. I'm crazy. *(flips finger on lower lip)* Bleah-bleah-bleah.

NURSE:
(enters) All right, Miss Carlyle, time's up. *(wraps towel around her)*

CARLYLE:
I'll stay longer. I don't mind.

NURSE:
No no, Miss Carlyle, we think you've had enough. We don't want to overdo the treatment. *(guides her off)*

FRANCES:
What about me?!

NURSE:

    (ignores her) *(leaves with MISS CARLYLE)*

FRANCES:

    (bangs on tub) **WHAT ABOUT ME!!**

SCENE 4

A man (ALFRED) writes a letter. His face is not seen by the audience.

ALFRED:

"Dear Miss Farmer,
I read all about your nervous breakdown and I just wanted to write and say that I think you're swell. I have seen all your movies. You are the most beautiful woman in the world. Please get better soon. You have more friends than you know.
Your devoted fan,
Alfred Knobble."

SCENE 5

FRANCES and MISS CARLYLE are in cots. A NURSE enters.

NURSE:
Good morning, Miss Carlyle.

CARLYLE:
Hello, Nursie. Do I get my shock today?

NURSE:
No. No, we've decided that you don't need shock for a while.

CARLYLE:
Oh. Well, whatever you think is best.

NURSE:
Did you have a nice sleep?

CARLYLE:
Oh yes, I had lovely dreams, too. All about mermaids and princes and sea captains.

NURSE:
(pulls back sheet) Miss Carlyle! You're all bruised!

CARLYLE:
Oh.

FRANCES:
She got raped again. Same orderly. Though I guess since it happens every night, it's now become a relationship.

NURSE:
(to MISS CARLYLE) Well for Heaven's Sake, why didn't you say something?

CARLYLE:

I thought it was treatment.

FRANCES:

Oh no, not unless a doctor does it.

NURSE:

(ignores FRANCES) (to MISS CARLYLE) Dr. Betelgeuse has decided that you've made a marked improvement and you're ready to go home.

FRANCES:

WHAT!

CARLYLE:

Oh Goody!

FRANCES:

That nutcase! Ready to go home?!

NURSE:

Really, Miss Farmer, if you were as well behaved as Miss Carlyle, you could leave, too.

CARLYLE:

(to NURSE) Don't tell her.

FRANCES:

Oh Christ! Of course!

CARLYLE:

(to FRANCES) No, no, don't do it. You're not ready. You'll get sent back and it will be far worse for you. *(to NURSE)* She's not ready.

NURSE:

Don't worry, Miss Carlyle. She's not going anywhere. Now, let's go get your things. *(guides her off)*

CARLYLE:

> *(to FRANCES)* Please, wait. Don't do it, yet.

FRANCES:

> Have a wonderful time in the outside world, Miss Carlyle. And many thanks for all you've done for me. You've been very helpful.

CARLYLE:

> You'll go to Hell! They'll send you to Hell!

NURSE:

> Miss Carlyle! What a thing to say!

SCENE 6

FRANCES FARMER in electric shock therapy. She is lying on a table. Her body is twitching. The ORDERLY turns off the current and removes the electrodes.

FRANCES:
(sits up, stretches arms) Ah—gee, that feels great!

ORDERLY:
Are you all right?

FRANCES:
Of course, I'm just hunky dory. Nothing like a good electroshock to get one going in the morning.

ORDERLY:
Are you being sarcastic?

FRANCES:
No. Of course not.

ORDERLY:
Cause if you don't like it, we'll do it again.

FRANCES:
No—really. It's fine. I feel terrific. Just point me in the direction of my ward.

ORDERLY:
You can't leave yet. Your doctor wants to see you.

FRANCES:
That will be nice. Have I seen him before?

ORDERLY:
Three times.

FRANCES:
Funny, I can't remember any of them. What's his name?

ORDERLY:
Dr. Betelgeuse.

FRANCES:
Oh. That will be nice. I can hardly wait.

DR. BETELGEUSE enters. He wears a polka-dot tie.

BETELGEUSE:
Hello, Frances.

FRANCES:
Hello, Dr. Betelgeuse. That's a very nice tie you're
wearing.

BETELGEUSE:
(to ORDERLY) Is she being sarcastic?

ORDERLY:
I don't know.

BETELGEUSE:
(to FRANCES) Are you being sarcastic?

FRANCES:
No, Dr. Betelgeuse.

*BETELGEUSE motions for the ORDERLY to leave. He
leaves.*

BETELGEUSE:
Do you like it here?

FRANCES:
Oh yes, Dr. Betelgeuse. Everyone is very nice, here.

BETELGEUSE:
   Everyone?

FRANCES:
   Yes.

BETELGEUSE:
   Do you think you're ready to leave here, yet?

FRANCES:
   Do you?

BETELGEUSE:
   Now Frances, I asked you first.

FRANCES:
   But you're the doctor and you know best.

BETELGEUSE:
   Don't you have any thoughts about it?

FRANCES:
   No, Dr. Betelgeuse. I have no thoughts.

BETELGEUSE:
   Would you like to see your mother?

FRANCES:
   Oh yes, I'd love to see my mother. I want to tell her how
   sorry I am for being bad.

BETELGEUSE:
   The nurses think you've made a marked improvement.
   You're not objecting to therapy, anymore.

FRANCES:
   Therapy is good for me. It's curing me.

BETELGEUSE:

> That's what I'm not sure about. You seem to be cured. But
> I can still detect some latent aggression

FRANCES:

> Oh no, Doctor.

BETELGEUSE:

> Maybe, we should take you off electroshock for a while.
> Just to see if you start acting up again. What do you think
> about that?

FRANCES:

> Whatever you think is best.

BETELGEUSE:

> *(looks at her)* Christ! What happened to your lip!

FRANCES:

> My lip?

BETELGEUSE:

> Your lower lip. It's all chewed off. Are you biting yourself?
> Is that what's happening? Transferring your aggression to
> self-mutilation.

FRANCES:

> I don't know what you're saying, Doctor, but the reason my
> lip is this way is because I was left in hydro by mistake for a
> long long time.

BETELGEUSE:

> What?!

FRANCES:

> I'm sure it wasn't anyone's fault. But I got very cold and I
> chewed my lip because I was so cold my teeth were
> chattering. I'm sorry I almost chewed my lip off, Doctor. I
> won't do it again.

BETELGEUSE:

Maybe we should take you off hydro. Although I don't know. Taking you off hydro and shock might be too drastic. We'll keep you on both, but reduce the treatments. That's it. That's what we'll do.

FRANCES:

Whatever you think is best, Doctor.

BETELGEUSE:

Well, we're not infallible, you know. *(starts to leave)* We do make mistakes.

FRANCES:

Yes. I know.

SCENE 7

LILLIAN, alone on stage.

LILLIAN:
Dear Mr. Knobble,
Thank you for your concern. Please do not believe all those stories you've been reading about me. They are all part of a vicious smear campaign. The truth is—*(pause)* I have contracted a mild form of tuberculosis and am presently convalescing. I will be better shortly and back on the silver screen in a brand new film- co-starring with *(flips through magazine)* Clark Gable. Tell all your friends.
Your favourite star, *(signs with a flourish)*
Frances Farmer.

SCENE 8

A NURSE brings FRANCES in to see DR. BETELGEUSE.

BETELGEUSE:
Well Frances, we're very proud of you. You've made a lot of progress and you're ready to go home.

FRANCES:
Home.

BETELGEUSE:
Don't you want to go home?

FRANCES:
Oh yes. But if I wanted to go somewhere else, could I go there, too?

BETELGEUSE:
You'd have to ask your mother. She's your guardian, now.

FRANCES:
My guardian?

BETELGEUSE:
You see, you're on parole. So, you're out of Steilacoom but you're under your mother's supervision.

FRANCES:
Parole.

BETELGEUSE:
Is something wrong, Frances?

FRANCES:
Sorry. Nothing's wrong. Oh, I'm so excited to be going home. Of course, I'll be sorry to leave all you nice people. Say goodbye to Frank the Orderly for me. He used to visit me every night. Of course, I didn't use to like it and now I

think I'll miss Frank. Even though his breath was awful and his thingee stank.

BETELGEUSE:
Thingee?

FRANCES:
You know.

BETELGEUSE:
What! This is outrageous! *(to NURSE)* Get Frank!

FRANCES:
Can I go now?

BETELGEUSE:
Frances, your name's going to go down in all our journals. You represent a significant victory for the mental hygiene movement.

FRANCES:
That's nice. Can I go now?

SCENE 9

Seattle, the Farmer home. FRANCES, LILLIAN and ERNEST.

FRANCE:
    Hi, Mamma.

LILLIAN:
    Little sister! *(runs up and hugs her)* I've missed you. I'm so glad you're all better. Let me look at you. *(stands back)* Oh dear. *(hands FRANCES a dress)* I bought you this. Put this on.

> *FRANCES looks at it blankly. LILLIAN starts to help her get dressed.*

FRANCES:
    Hi, Dad.

ERNEST:
    Hi, Frannie.

LILLIAN:
    You don't look very good. Your hair's a mess and you've gained weight. I hope you can fit into that dress. Let's see. Better comb your hair. *(gets comb, starts combing hair)*

FRANCES:
    OW! It's okay, Mamma. We don't need to comb my hair right away.

LILLIAN:
    That dress is bit tight, but it'll do.

FRANCES:
    Do for what?

LILLIAN:

Now, we'll just fix your hair. *(LILLIAN puts FRANCES' hair up in a french roll while she talks)* The boys should be here any minute.

FRANCES:

The boys?!

LILLIAN:

The reporters. I've called a press conference.

FRANCES:

What!

LILLIAN:

For your comeback.

FRANCES:

Mamma, I just got home.

LILLIAN:

We can't waste a minute getting you back into circulation. You're thirty years old. That's almost over the hill for Hollywood.

FRANCES:

What if I don't want to go back?

LILLIAN:

I'd hate to see you have another attack, dear. The staff at Steilacoom said you were completely cured.

FRANCES:

Mamma, do you have any idea of what goes on there?

LILLIAN:

When you were delusional, you told me all sorts of dreadful stories. But let's forget about all that. We can go back to being a team again.

FRANCES:
A team.

LILLIAN:
I only want what's best for my little sister. Now, just put
some lipstick on. Your lower lip looks very odd.

The doorbell rings.

LILLIAN:
Oh! They're here! *(answers door)* Come in, come in. I'm so
glad you could make it.

REPORTERS crowd in, taking pictures.

LILLIAN:
Frances is just ecstatic to be home again, aren't you, dear?

FRANCES:
Yes, Mamma.

REPORTER 1:
Welcome back, Miss Farmer.

Someone takes a picture.

REPORTER 2:
Tell me, Miss Farmer, how does it feel to be back in the
real world?

FRANCES:
It's very nice, thank you. I've always liked the real world.

REPORTER 1:
What we really want to know, Miss Farmer, is will we be
seeing you back in the movies again?

FRANCES:
(looks at LILLIAN) I certainly hope so.

REPORTER 2:
    What exactly happened, Miss Farmer? What exactly drove
    you over the edge?

FRANCES:
    (smiles) Overwork.

REPORTER 2:
    And how did you find your experience at Steilacoom?

FRANCES:
    Well—the conditions there are absolutely barbar—

LILLIAN:
    Miraculous! Just miraculous the way they restored my
    daughter to her rightful self.

FRANCES:
    Yes, it's amazing what 130 volts of elec—

LILLIAN:
    TIME FOR FAN MAIL! *(hands FRANCES a huge stack)* Okay,
    okay, sit down, Frances. Open the letter. *(to REPORTER
    with camera)* Now, stand on her left. No—not on her right.
    That's her bad side. Right there. Now, smile for the
    camera, Frances. OOOOPS! Don't take a picture yet. You
    just need a bit of lipstick.

FRANCES:
    Hide the scars, Mamma?

LILLIAN:
    (laughs nervously) Right. Just put a little there. *(puts lipstick
    on FRANCES' lip)* Now, read the letter. *(to REPORTER)* And
    take the picture. GO!

    REPORTER takes the picture.

LILLIAN:

Good, good. I want that in the paper. Fan mail is the life blood of an actress, isn't it, Frances?

FRANCES:

Yes, Mamma.

LILLIAN:

If you stop getting it, you know you're through.

FRANCES:

That's true.

REPORTER 2:

Well, judging by the pile of letters, I'd say your career was well underway again.

FRANCES:

Thank you. And keep those cards and letters coming. It's been a swell interview. *(ushers REPORTERS out)*

REPORTER 1:

But we still have a few more questions.

FRANCES:

(smiles) And it's been a pleasure answering them. *(still ushering them out)* Thank you very much. And thank you, Mamma, for organizing this little welcome home party for me. *(kisses her on the cheek)*

   REPORTER takes a picture.

FRANCES:

And now, I think I'll have a little nap. I had lots of naps at Steilacoom, Mamma. It's a habit I've developed.

LILLIAN:

Well, I guess she's tired. I'll answer your questions.

REPORTER 1:
Nah, it's okay. Thanks Mrs. Farmer.

REPORTER 2:
Yeah, thanks. Goodbye. *(they leave)*

LILLIAN:
(follows them out) Really, anything at all. I know just as much about Frances as she does.

FRANCES grabs her father.

FRANCES:
Why didn't you do anything! Why did you let her do that to me!!

ERNEST:
Let go of me, Frannie.

FRANCES:
What? Scared of your crazy daughter. I'm a lot crazier now than I was before. Why didn't you do something!

ERNEST:
She had herself declared sole guardian.

FRANCES:
You could have fought it. You could have stood up for me.

ERNEST:
I saw the welts on her arms. I read those transcripts. The Frances I knew wouldn't have done those things.

FRANCES:
The Frances you knew hadn't been locked up and tortured.

ERNEST:
Your mother has plans. Try and get along with her.

FRANCES:
And be a fucking doormat like you. No thank you!

ERNEST:
Don't swear. She won't like it.

FRANCES:
(moves away from him)

ERNEST:
I love you, Frannie.

FRANCES:
It's not doing me much good, Dad.

SCENE 10

DR. BETELGEUSE and DR. NICHOLSON.

NICHOLSON:

> *(walks up to BETELGEUSE and throw newspaper at him)*
> Cured, eh!

BETELGEUSE:

> *(looks at it)* Oh.

NICHOLSON:

> This is her fifth escape.

BETELGEUSE:

> I guess she doesn't like staying with her mother.

NICHOLSON:

> Read the paper, you clot! She's been at two sets of relatives.
> Escaped both times. We pronounced her cured! A medical
> landmark and the goddamned woman's running around
> like a lunatic! Picking grapes in California!!

BETELGEUSE:

> Maybe we should let her pick grapes. Schizophrenics are
> very good at menial tasks.

NICHOLSON:

> Yeah yeah, I know. Schizophrenics built the pyramids.

BETELGEUSE:

> Well, the bicameral mind...

NICHOLSON:

> Shut up!!

BETELGEUSE:

> I just don't understand it. She was so calm and well-
> adjusted.

142

NICHOLSON:

She's an actress, nimblenut.

BETELGEUSE:

Excuse me, Dr. Nicholson, could you please call me by my correct name?

NICHOLSON:

The woman has tricked you. She simply pretended to be well-adjusted. She's made a laughing stock of us!

BETELGEUSE:

We could ask her mother to re-commit her.

NICHOLSON:

Her mother doesn't want to re-commit her. Her mother still hopes she'll go back to Hollywood.

BETELGEUSE:

She can't go back to work. Her schizophrenic tendencies—

NICHOLSON:

Yeah yeah, I know. Believe me, I know all about schizophrenics. I'm tired of hearing about them. Convention after convention and all we ever talk about are schizophrenics. I'm fed to the teeth with schizophrenics. The woman's a goddamn lunatic and that's all there is to it! So, you know what to do.

BETELGEUSE:

Do?

NICHOLSON:

One of our aircraft is missing, nimblenut. I want it returned! *(exits)*

SCENE 11

Darkness. LILLIAN, sitting in a chair.

FRANCES:

(enters) (turns on light) Mama! Are you all right? Why are you staring at me? I just went out for a few hours. You weren't around so—

LILLIAN:

The Doctor called me. You're never going back to Hollywood, are you? You've tricked me.

FRANCES:

What are you talking about?

LILLIAN:

You're just pretending to be normal. You'll never be the same.

FRANCES:

Then let me go. Let me live my own life.

LILLIAN:

It's too late, little sister. It's just too late. When I look at you, now, I don't know what I see. I don't know who you are.

TWO MEN IN WHITE COATS arrive at the door. They take FRANCES.

FRANCES:

(struggling) Goddammit! You goddamn bitch! You fucking—

LILLIAN:

The devil has entered into you, little sister and there's nothing you or I can do about it.

FRANCES:

Why are you doing this to me, Mamma?

LILLIAN:

(sits in chair) Because, once upon a time, little sister, you were beautiful. *(she weeps)*

SCENE 12

Ward D. Darkness. Huddled bodies. TWO MEN sneak in.
No one takes notice.

*A NOTE ON WARD D:
This was a large barrack at the back of Steilacoom where
incurables were put. Eating, sleeping and defecating were
conducted on the floor. Patients were naked most of the time.
Food was thrown in a large slop pile and patients had to
fight for it. Every month, the patients were lined up against a
wall and hosed down.

MAN 1 (GORDO):
> Which one is she?

MAN:
> Jesus! How should I know. They all look like hell. *(calls to*
> *MATRON)* Pssst! Where's the movie star! We paid good
> money and we want a movie star.

MATRON:
> Keep it down, guys.

MAN:
> We don't want no psycho who thinks she's a movie star.

MATRON:
> The money was for sneaking you in here. It's a dollar extra
> for the movie star.

GORDO:
> There's no movie star here.

MATRON:
> You never heard of Frances Farmer?

MAN:
> Frances Farmer?! Geez, Gordo, you ever see her in 'Son of
> Fury?' She was terrific. *(pays MATRON)* Where is she?

MATRON:

Over there. *(points to FRANCES who is lying in a heap on the floor)*

GORDO:

Will she attack us?

MAN:

Don't be such a chickenshit, Gordo.

MATRON:

They've juiced her up. She's in the ozone right now. *(leaves)*

MAN:

Come on. *(goes over to FRANCES)* Hey, little lady, time for action. *(climbs on her)*

FRANCES:

The Lord is my shepherd I shall not want. He maketh me to lie down in piles of deep shit...

MAN:

You bet, baby. Now shut up.

FRANCES:

He leadeth me beside the stinking sewers.

> *They rape her in darkness. CLIFFORD ODETS appears to FRANCES.*

ODETS:

So, you've joined the kingdom of the damned?

FRANCES:

I am my own Kingdom.

ODETS:

You've never been in love before, have you, Saint Frances?

FRANCES:
Please. Go away.

ODETS:
You've never known what it's like to completely surrender yourself to another person.

FRANCES:
Surrender isn't love.

ODETS:
It's a saving grace. If you totally abandoned yourself, you'd be protected. But you're holding back a small portion of self-esteem and that's the part that will get infected.

FRANCES:
Infected?

GORDO:
Geezus? Do you think she's got the clap?

ODETS:
Didn't you know? This is the century of the virus. Silent infection followed by complete interior rot.

FRANCES:
Am I going mad? Is this what it's like?

ODETS:
Do you love me, Saint Frances?

FRANCES:
No. No. I don't love you. Go away.

ODETS:
You should. You should love your fellow man. Reclaim your light.

FRANCES:
What?

ODETS:
Reclaim the light that's yours. *(leaves)*

The MAN and GORDO stand up.

MAN:
Thanks little lady. *(drops some coins on her)*

FRANCES:
(studies coins) My light. *(muses)* My light has been stolen.

MATRON:
(passing by) Get used to it, sister. Can't deny the boys their Saturday nights. *(sees coins)* Hey, they paid you?! Gimme that!

FRANCES:
Can I kiss your foot, Matron?

MATRON:
You're a real loop the loop. Sure, go ahead.

FRANCES:
(kissing foot) I'm just so grateful that you haven't shown one of my old films. When I was in Ward A, they used to do that to torture me.

MATRON:
Really? Which film?

FRANCES:
'Come and Get it.' That one upset me the most.

MATRON:
(smiles) Really? *(leaves)*

FRANCES:

   (exultant) Yes! Yes! Sometimes it can be so pathetically easy.

SCENE 13

*Ward D. Frances' film 'Come and Get It' is being shown to
the inmates. The film is at the part where Frances playing a
young innocent girl sings 'Auralie,'* (or you could show the
part earlier in the film when Frances' character Lotta sings
the song.) One FEMALE PATIENT is sobbing throughout.
Calls of "Down in front," "Shaddap, I can't hear nutthin."
etc. FRANCES sits as close as possible to the film. She is
bathed in its light. She is rocking and chanting amid the
general din.*

FRANCES:
> *(chanting)* Come on, Baby. Come to Mamma. Come on
> Baby, come to Mamma. Come on, *(stretches her arms out to
> film)* come on, come on...*(builds to a crescendo ending in)*
> YES! YES! YES! YES YES!

> *The projector breaks down. FRANCES stands up, with her
> arms outstretched. The palms of her hands are glowing. She
> slowly walks around the room. She sings and finishes the
> song that was interrupted on screen. FRANCES approaches
> the sobbing FEMALE PATIENT. The other PATIENTS and
> the NURSES watch her, transfixed. FRANCES leans down to
> the woman and gently places her glowing palm on the
> woman's forehead. The FEMALE PATIENT abruptly stops
> sobbing. She looks up and smiles at FRANCES. FRANCES
> looks at her glowing hands.*

> **'Auralie' is the same tune as 'Love Me Tender.'*

SCENE 14

Ward D. Darkness. One can vaguely make out bodies of men and women crawling about.

FRANCES:
The revolution against God shall begin in Ward D.

PATIENT:
Hey Saint Frances!

FRANCES:
They call me Saint Frances. I try not to let it go to my head. *(opens Bible which she is carrying)* The remaining privilege of the incarcerated. *(looks up, brandishes Bible at the ceiling)* Know thy enemy. *(laughs)* Hey God, I'm using your own words against you! You're an absentee landlord and you want me to do your work for you. Well, I'll do it. I'll make them all sane and we'll start an insurrection. The meek shall inherit the earth all right. Over your dead body.

PATIENT:
(tugs at her leg) Sing to me, Saint Frances.

FRANCES:
(sings to the tune of 'My Kind of Town') "My kind of ward. The Hell Hole is my kind of ward."

The other patients join in.

MATRON'S VOICE :
SHUT UP IN THERE!

FRANCES:
(shouts back) WHY? BECAUSE WE'RE HAVING FUN? BECAUSE WE'RE HAVING A LIFE? *(sings)* "My kind of ward, the Hell Hole is...My kind of ward..

PATIENTS:

> (with FRANCES) My kind of ward! (they continue singing)

FRANCES:

> The revolution begins here! Who wants enlightenment?

PATIENTS:

> I do! I do!

FRANCES:

> Okay okay, come on over.

> *The PATIENTS crawl over.*

FRANCES:

> Don't crawl. One of the first rules of enlightenment is—
> you are a human being so you don't crawl. You stand erect.

> *FRANCES lifts up some of the PATIENTS. She puts her*
> *hands to their foreheads. They act as though they are receiv-*
> *ing some rare form of energy. They move away, slightly dazed.*
> *They mutter things like this to themselves.*

PATIENT 1:

> My name is Mary Morgenthal. I live at 559 Bloomfield
> Crescent. I was once possessed by demons but I'm ready to
> go home now. I feel fine. (etc. adlib)

PATIENT 2:

> Where am I? What am I doing here? Where am I?

PATIENT 3:

> Ralph Blankenstein. Chartered Accountant. It's tax time.
> Ralph Blankenstein...(etc.adlib)

PATIENT 4:

> My God! The children! I have to pick them up for school.
> (etc. adlib)

Other PATIENTS that FRANCES has not laid hands on, stagger around and fall over. A Woman (MISS CARLYLE) enters quietly. She goes around touching the PATIENTS that FRANCES has touched.

CARLYLE:
You are drawing attention to yourself.

FRANCES:
Miss Carlyle?! You work here?

When MISS CARLYLE touches one of FRANCES' "cured" PATIENTS, that patient reverts to his/her former misery, but much sedated.

CARLYLE:
In the other wards, yes. It's a very good job and I like it. You must stop defying Him.

FRANCES:
It's just a hobby. You see, He doesn't really exist.

CARLYLE:
He does exist and He will punish you.

FRANCES:
I'm in the bowels of the earth. He'd have a hell of a time finding me.

CARLYLE:
You're using your powers for your own vanity.

FRANCES:
It doesn't last as long as I'd like. But they're pretty coherent for an hour or so. If I keep at it—*(muses)* Here, let me lay one on you. Maybe I can get you to quit your job. *(holds out her hand to touch MISS CARLYLE's forehead)*

CARLYLE:

(backs away) You must stop this!

FRANCES:

(laughs) Make me! I dare Him to make me stop!

> MISS CARLYLE leaves. The PATIENTS that FRANCES has
> "enlightened" realize that they have things to do at home and
> want to leave. They start muttering things like, "I gotta get
> out of here. I gotta get home. Let's go, etc." Their muttering
> gets louder until they are shouting, "I gotta get out! I WANT
> OUT!!" The MATRON walks in.

MATRON:

WHAT THE HELL IS GOING ON IN HERE!

> The PATIENTS try and rush out past her. The MATRON
> blows a whistle which she has around her neck. ORDERLIES
> rush in and push the PATIENTS away from the MATRON.

MATRON:

It's that Farmer bitch again. Give her a needle.

ORDERLIES:

Of what?

MATRON:

Who cares!

> The ORDERLIES and the MATRON struggle with
> FRANCES. The PATIENTS watch, cowed.

FRANCES:

There is the brain. And there is the mind. The brain is
purely physical. You could cut my head open and you
could see my brain. But you can never see my mind. And
that's the part that works. (chants in the manner of a prophet
while the MATRON and ORDERLIES pin her down to the
ground and give her a needle) There is the Brain and there is

the Mind. And in the seat of the Mind, there is the Will. And in the seat of the Will, there is the Soul. Power of refusal! *(kicks out at the ORDERLIES)* I REFUSE!! You can twist my brain inside out! I WILL it back into place. There is nothing you can do to me. You will not conquer me. Hey God, was Lucifer a woman? *(passes out)*

> *The ORDERLIES and MATRON carry FRANCES to another area and dump her in a pile on the floor.*

SCENE 15

DR. NICHOLSON, DR. BETELGEUSE and DR. FREEMAN, a visiting doctor. DR. FREEMAN is wearing a sleeveless white operating jacket. He is bald, has a dome-shaped head, sports a small moustache and a goatee and wears round wire-rimmed glasses. He bears some resemblance to Clifford Odets.

NICHOLSON:

Betelgeuse, this is Dr. Freeman. He is looking over our facilities. He's particularly interested in Farmer.

FREEMAN:

I hear you're still having problems with her.

BETELGEUSE:

Nothing that we can't handle.

FREEMAN:

She's been encouraging the other patients to rebel?

BETELGEUSE:

We've put her under sedation.

NICHOLSON:

Fat lot of good that does.

FREEMAN:

What about shock?

NICHOLSON:

She loves shock. She lives on shock.

BETELGEUSE:

She's made some progress.

NICHOLSON:

Come off it, Doctor. She's a holy terror.

BETELGEUSE:
    But—

FREEMAN:
    Your approach is outdated. You're going from the outside
    in. We must rectify the situation from the inside out.
    Repair the physiological malformation.

NICHOLSON:
    Lobotomy?

FREEMAN:
    Psychosurgery.

BETELGEUSE:
    Quite a high failure rate.

FREEMAN:
    This is a totally new approach. 90% effective.

BETELGEUSE:
    What about the ten percent? Her parents—

FREEMAN:
    And it is undetectable. It leaves no visible scar.

NICHOLSON & BETELGEUSE:
    Oh.

FREEMAN:
    The operation only takes two minutes. We go in through
    the eyelid and sever the nerve connecting the cortex with
    the thalamus. A simple procedure. Brain and motor
    functions are still intact. The patient can walk, talk, eat,
    sleep and generally function as a normal human being.

BETELGEUSE:
    "Generally" function?

FREEMAN:
There is some loss in the patient's imaginative power. But that is what we want to do. Frances Farmer is sick in her imagination. We are releasing her from the slavery of her diseased thoughts.

BETELGEUSE:
It seems too drastic. Too risky.

NICHOLSON:
We were hoping you'd approve, but as you have no authority in this matter, your objections are irrelevant.

BETELGEUSE:
She's my patient. What do you mean I have no authority?!

FREEMAN:
I've been put in charge. You've made no contribution to the field. No new research. I have developed a technique that will revolutionize the science. How dare you stand in my way. I say, let there be hope for Frances Farmer.

(pulls out icepick)

SCENE 16

FRANCES, alone on stage.

FRANCES:
    I keep having this dream. I dream I'm with this woman and she's asking me questions and I don't remember anything so I can't answer her questions. Then, she starts showing me people and I'm supposed to know who they are. But I don't. I don't remember who they are. And she brings more people and more people till finally she brings this man and I don't know who he is, either. He's bald and he wears glasses and he has a big nose with hairs growing out of it. And he's wearing a white jacket with no sleeves and he's got hairs all over his arms and his fingers. And he raises his hand and he's got a long thin icepick in it and he brings it up to my eye. And then he brings out a little wooden mallet and he taps on the icepick and he plunges the icepick right into my eye. And just as he does that—I suddenly remember who these people are. So I say—Stop! Stop! I remember them. I do! Honest. They're my family and I love them. But after he's done that, I can't love them, anymore. I can't love anyone anymore.

    The sound of a wooden mallet hitting an icepick.
    Lights down on FRANCES.

SCENE 17

ERNEST, LILLIAN and Dr. Betelgeuse. LILLIAN is in a wheelchair and ERNEST is pushing it.

BETELGEUSE:
Well well well, Mrs. Farmer, Mr. Farmer. I'm sure you never expected to see your daughter well again, but by some miracle of coincidence—she recovered at almost exactly the same moment that you had your stroke, Mrs. Farmer.

LILLIAN:
(enraged) Miracle!! You call having a stroke a miracle!!!

BETELGEUSE:
No—well—what I meant was—

ERNEST:
Lillian, just calm down. Don't get excited. *(to DR. BETELGEUSE)* She's become a little testy since—

LILLIAN:
If anyone deserves a stroke, it's that worthless bitch! What's she ever done for anyone. Dick!

ERNEST:
Obscenities—after she had the stroke—

BETELGEUSE:
Usually, with stroke victims, the speech as well as the motor functions are impaired.

ERNEST:
Yes—well, not in her case. If anything, they've been heightened.

LILLIAN:
Stop talking about me as though I'm not here. I'm here goddammit! I'M RIGHT HERE IN FRONT OF YOU!!!

161

BETELGEUSE:
>
> We're well aware of that, Mrs. Farmer. Now please calm down. Your daughter is well enough to come home and look after you.

LILLIAN:
>
> It's about time she did something useful.

BETELGEUSE:
>
> *(looks around)* Oh—here she is.

> *Nurse CARLYLE brings FRANCES in. FRANCES has a cheerful expression on her face. FRANCES now has a habit of rubbing her hands together as though trying to find something. (I leave it to the discretion of the actress to do this occasionally through the following "post-lobotomy" scenes)*

FRANCES:
>
> Hi, Mom.

LILLIAN:
>
> Hi, Frances.

FRANCES:
>
> Hi, Mom.

ERNEST:
>
> Frances?

FRANCES:
>
> *(looks at him)* Hi, Pop.

ERNEST:
>
> Pop? She never used to call me "Pop."

BETELGEUSE:
>
> It's been a long time since she's seen you.

LILLIAN:
    Come on. Let's go.

ERNEST:
    Frances, are you all right?

FRANCES:
    Yes, Pop, I'm just fine, thank you very much. And you?

ERNEST:
    I'm okay. Your mother's had a stroke.

FRANCES:
    (slowly) O-k-a-a-a-y.

LILLIAN:
    She could care less.

ERNEST:
    What's that book in her hand?

BETELGEUSE:
    Oh—well—ah—it's a Bible, isn't it, Frances?

FRANCES:
    (points at Bible) (smiles) I'm a faceless sinner.

ERNEST:
    Jesus Christ! What have you done to her?

FRANCES:
    (stares at ground) I've been a bad girl.

ERNEST:
    What's wrong with her? You've done something to her!

BETELGEUSE:
    Really, Mr. Farmer, need I remind you that you and Mrs.
    Farmer authorized our treatments for your daughter. She

is a bit subdued at the moment, possibly the shock of returning home, but I assure you, she'll recover presently.

ERNEST:
You mean, she's not cured.

BETELGEUSE:
No—no, I didn't mean that. What I meant was—she will soon return to her old self.

LILLIAN:
But she was crazy, then.

BETELGEUSE:
I mean—before she became crazy. That old self.

FRANCES:
(raises arms) I'm guilty. Oh Lord, I'm guilty.

ERNEST:
You're sure about this.

BETELGEUSE:
Mr. Farmer, do you want your daughter back or not?

ERNEST:
She just seems—sort of weird.

BETELGEUSE:
I assure, she's quite harmless.

LILLIAN:
Thank you, Dr. Betelgeuse. Frances!

FRANCES:
Yes.

LILLIAN:
You're coming home. Push my chair.

FRANCES:

(pushes LILLIAN's chair) (chants) I'M GUILTY. OH LORD, I'M GUILTY.

They leave.

* A NOTE ON LOBOTOMIZED PATIENTS

The best description of a lobotomized person is in an article written by Irving Wallace, called "The Man Without a Conscience." It is in the book 'The Sunday Gentleman,' which is a collection of articles written by Wallace from 1950 to 1965. His article is about a man who chose to have a lobotomy. It describes in great detail, the man's behaviour before and after the lobotomy. Wallace later wrote a postscript in 1963 to describe further changes.

The important points which I gleaned from my research and which are critical to playing these "post-lobotomy" scenes are:
1. The patient is cheerful and has a childlike manner.
2. The patient has a loud voice which seems out of place in its surroundings.
3. The patient is free of social inhibitions. A person who is recently lobotomized might urinate in someone's home.
4. A lobotomized person behaves like a very dull and unimaginative ten-year-old child.
5. The man in Wallace's article became very gregarious and eccentric.

The actress should not take the dull monotone "zombie" approach. It is very boring to watch. The scenes work better if the actress is childlike and cheerful. When FRANCES flings her arms up and says "I'm guilty, O Lord, I'm guilty," she should do this as if she's a child imitating an action that someone showed her.

SCENE 18

FRANCES and her mother. LILLIAN is in a wheelchair.

LILLIAN:
Did you sweep the floor?

FRANCES:
Yes, Mamma.

LILLIAN:
It doesn't look swept to me. What's that? *(points)*

FRANCES:
Dirt, Mamma.

LILLIAN:
Well, pick it up.

FRANCES:
(starts to pick it up with her hands)

LILLIAN:
Not with your hands! The dustpan.

FRANCES:
Yes, Mamma.

LILLIAN:
It's out in the kitchen. Go get it. And get the broom too.

FRANCES:
(leaves)

LILLIAN:
(to FRANCES in kitchen) You ruined my life you know,
Frances. You ruined your life, too. You had no right to do
that. You and those Goddamn Commies. *(fingers letter)*
Goddamn fan mail. I should let you read it some time.

That is, if you can still read. Can you still read, Cinderella?
I wish they'd just forget about you and leave us alone.

> *FRANCES returns. She stands behind LILLIAN. She is*
> *holding a large breadknife in her hand. LILLIAN does not*
> *know she is there.*

LILLIAN:

I don't know why you got so haughty. Anyone can be a star.
If I had your looks and your figure—

FRANCES:

(raises knife)

LILLIAN:

I could have been a star. Hey Cinderella! What's keeping
you?

FRANCES:

Who's Cinderella?

LILLIAN:

(turns around) Frances! What are you doing with that
knife?!

FRANCES:

Who's Cinderella?

LILLIAN:

(takes knife) She was a bad girl. *(slashes FRANCES skirt with*
knife) And all her fine clothes turned to rags. *(makes another*
slash in skirt) And that's all you need to know about
Cinderella. I think you'd better have some protein. The
doctor said you'd act funny if you didn't have your
protein. Did you eat that egg I put out for breakfast?

FRANCES:

No.

LILLIAN:

Frances! If you don't eat your egg—you won't get your protein. And if you don't get your protein, you're gonna start to act queer. And you know what'll happen if you act queer, dear.

FRANCES:

No.

LILLIAN:

We'll send you back.

FRANCES:

You'll send me back.

LILLIAN:

To Steilacoom. All bad girls go to Steilacoom.

FRANCES:

(hangs head) I'm a faceless sinner.

LILLIAN:

That you are, little sister. That you are. Now, go out to the kitchen and eat your egg.

FRANCES:

Yes, Mamma.

LILLIAN:

And Frances.

FRANCES:

Yes, Mamma?

LILLIAN:

Don't play jokes with breadknives. It's not funny.

FRANCES:

Yes, Mamma.

SCENE 19

FRANCES, her mother and her father. FRANCES is sitting in a chair off to one side. She stares off into space. ERNEST is rummaging around in the kitchen.

ERNEST:
> *(offstage amidst the sounds of lots of bottles being jangled)*
> There's nothing in the fridge but cream.

LILLIAN:
> I like cream.

ERNEST:
> *(offstage amidst sounds of cupboards slamming)* There's nothing in the cupboards but cream of wheat. Boxes of it.

LILLIAN:
> That's all we can afford right now. Besides, I like it.

ERNEST:
> *(comes out with a small bowl of gruel-like substance) (sits down to eat it, makes a face)*

LILLIAN:
> She came at me with a breadknife, today.

ERNEST:
> She did?

LILLIAN:
> Yeah. She's sitting there looking innocent as all get-out but she came at me, just the same.

ERNEST:
> Should we send her back?

LILLIAN:
> *(shrugs)* No point. She won't do it again.

ERNEST:

I'd like her to leave.

LILLIAN:

You would?

ERNEST:

Yes. There's a job posting at the Olympic hotel.

LILLIAN:

It can't be too complicated. Frances can't do anything that requires much thought.

ERNEST:

She'd fold towels and she'd sort laundry. Plus she gets free room and board.

LILLIAN:

You really don't want her around?

ERNEST:

(looks at FRANCES) No. I don't.

SCENE 20

Hotel room. A MAN and FRANCES are in bed.

MAN:

(takes a drag on his cigarette) For a shy chick, you don't waste any time. Oh wait—this isn't some new scam, is it? There isn't some goon outside—I mean—I don't have any money.

FRANCES:

I liked the movie.

MAN:

Tarzan? You liked Tarzan?

FRANCES:

Is that what his name was?

MAN:

Look, you're very pretty and very nice but you're weird.

FRANCES:

Weird?

MAN:

Yeah—you give me the creeps. Now, most women would get upset if I said something like that to them, but you just sit there and take it.

FRANCES:

I'm a faceless sinner.

MAN:

Well, that's going a bit far. I'd just say you're weird. I mean, did you enjoy it?

FRANCES:

It?

171

MAN:

> What we did just now.

FRANCES:

> Did we do something?

MAN:

> Forget it!

FRANCES:

> *(hangs her head)* I'm a faceless sinner.

MAN:

> You're a religious nut, aren't you. Look, I'm sorry. I didn't mean to upset you. It's just that the whole thing has left me feeling a bit strange. You're not a faceless sinner. You have a beautiful face. It's a very definite face. And you didn't sin. It was a non-event. I'm sure it wouldn't even qualify as a misdemeanor. If anyone sinned, I did. Why do I feel like a child molester? You're a consenting adult. I'm a consenting adult. Why do I feel like a child molester?

FRANCES:

> Tarzan.

SCENE 21

*FRANCES and another man (ALFRED) in bed. He has a
big fat nose.*

ALFRED:
You know, you've got a quality about you that's really
gentle. Soothing.

FRANCES:
Yes.

ALFRED:
You're a beautiful woman, Frances. So, I'm going to give
you some advice.

FRANCES:
Yes.

ALFRED:
You should stop fucking every guy that comes along.

FRANCES:
Oh. *(pause)* They ask me to do it.

ALFRED:
You should say, "No."

FRANCES:
I like to be beside bodies in the dark. It reminds me of
where I come from.

ALFRED:
Why don't you go live at home, then?

FRANCES:
No—not there.

ALFRED:
   Where?

FRANCES:
   I don't remember where. I just remember the feeling. It's
   warm and dark and there are bodies everywhere.

ALFRED:
   You're too good for them, Frances. Those guys don't care.
   They just think you're an easy lay. But I know you. You're a
   tortured soul, Frances.

FRANCES:
   What's your name again?

ALFRED:
   Jesus, Frances! Alfred. My name's Alfred.

FRANCES:
   I'm sorry, Alfred.

ALFRED:
   Do you know me? Do I register at all with you?

FRANCES:
   Yes. I know you.

ALFRED:
   Who am I to you, then?

FRANCES:
   You're the man with the big fat nose.

ALFRED:
   Frances, do you like me?

FRANCES:
   Yes, Alfred. I like you.

ALFRED:
    Frances, I'd like to marry you.

FRANCES:
    Why?

ALFRED:
    You need me. I understand your torture and I think I can
    help you. Please, marry me.

FRANCES:
    I don't think I'm allowed to.

ALFRED:
    Of course, you're allowed to. You can do anything you like.

FRANCES:
    Okay.

ALFRED:
    Really, Frances? You really want to marry me?!

FRANCES:
    Okay.

ALFRED:
    (*hugs her*) Oh Frances, you're so beautiful. You were so
    beautiful in 'Son of Fury.' Sort of amazing—a big lug like
    me married to a girl like you. Christ, you were beautiful.
    You're an angel.

FRANCES:
    (*smiles vacantly*) I'm a faceless sinner.

SCENE 22

ALFRED, alone on stage.

ALFRED:

I just couldn't believe my luck. All my life she was a princess to me. And I, Alfred Knobble, actually had a chance with the princess. There was a glowing inside of her. It was like she was under a spell and all I had to do was kiss her and wake her up and the glowing would come out again. I knew I had no business being with her. And if she was in her senses, she wouldn't look twice at me. But she was mine. I had her. She was every man's dream. How could I refuse?

SCENE 23

FRANCES is sitting in a chair, staring off into space.
ALFRED enters, takes off jacket, puts it on a chair.

ALFRED:
> *(clutching a bottle of whiskey, takes a swig, glares at FRANCES)*
> This is a nightmare. I'm living in a goddamn nightmare.

FRANCES:
> *(smiles)*

ALFRED:
> Stop smiling, you bitch!

FRANCES:
> *(stops smiling, lowers head)*

ALFRED:
> Jesus Christ! Stop doing everything I tell you. It doesn't matter what anyone tells you, you do it. I've seen you folding those towels. You'd keep doing it until someone told you to stop.

FRANCES:
> *(looks at him blankly)*

ALFRED:
> Do you think? Is there a mind in there?! I'm talking to you!!

FRANCES:
> Oh. *(pause)* Am I supposed to answer a question, Alfred?

ALFRED:
> YES!

FRANCES:
> What's the question, Alfred?

ALFRED:

> And stop calling me Alfred all the time. Alfred this. Alfred that. You only call me Alfred cause you wouldn't know who I was, otherwise. I'd be the man with the big fat nose.

FRANCES:

> You're the man with the big fat nose, Alfred?

ALFRED:

> AAAAH! *(clutches head)* *(sits for a moment, takes another swig)* I try and help you but it's useless. It's worse than being by myself. It's like living in a room with mirrors. Monkey see, monkey do.

FRANCES:

> I don't see a monkey, Alfred.

ALFRED:

> That vacant stupid expression. *(goes to FRANCES and slowly twists her face)* I'd like to take your face and mash it up. Your fucking face got me here.

FRANCES:

> Can I have a drink, Alfred? *(reaches for bottle)*

ALFRED:

> *(smacks her)* NO! Fucking alchie. I married a goddamn alcoholic.

FRANCES:

> *(cowers)* Why can't I have a drink, Alfred?

ALFRED:

> 'Cause you'll get drunk and believe it or not, you're even more stupid when you're drunk.

FRANCES:

> Is that bad, Alfred?

ALFRED:

Stop calling me Alfred!

FRANCES:

Can I go home?

ALFRED:

You're here. This is home. And you can only stay here if you're good and if you're not good, guess where you'll go.

FRANCES:

Where?

ALFRED:

Steilacoom. I'll send you back to Steilacoom.

FRANCES:

(whimpers) No please, no please, don't send me back to Steilacoom.

ALFRED:

Do you even know where it is! Do you even know what it is!

FRANCES:

(whimpers, crawls on floor) No please, don't send me back to Steilacoom.

ALFRED:

Where is it, then? What's Steilacoom?

FRANCES:

It's—it's—oh, it's a bad place. I think.

ALFRED:

YOU THINK! You grovelling snivelling idiot! You don't even know why you're grovelling. You just got used to grovelling! *(boots her)*

FRANCES:
No please. *(curls up in ball)*

ALFRED:
(boots her again) (leaves)

FRANCES:
(looks up) (crawls to his coat, reaches in pockets for wallet, pulls out money, puts on hat and coat) (leaves)

SCENE 24

FRANCES with hat and coat on, carrying liquor bottles in brown paper bag. She is followed by a man wearing a loud plaid suit (ROY DICKSELL.) He wears a hat with a large brim, which partially conceals his face.

DICKSELL:
Frances!

FRANCES:
(turns around)

DICKSELL:
I was right. You're Frances Farmer, aren't you.

FRANCES:
No. *(starts to run away)*

DICKSELL:
(catches her) I thought Geez! That sure looks like Frances Farmer. Boy oh boy, this is my lucky day.

FRANCES breaks away from him. She runs but drops her bottles. They break. She stops and looks at them.

FRANCES:
They're broken.

DICKSELL:
I'll buy some more for you. Please. I insist. You know, I've been a big fan of yours for years. In face, you inspired me to go into the Biz. I thought, Geez, if I could work with broads—er—I mean-dames like that—boy would I be in the cat's patootie—know what I mean?

FRANCES:
No.

181

DICKSELL:

> You're a class act, boy. Name's Dicksell. Roy Dicksell. "Sell!" Get it? *(holds out hand)*

FRANCES:

> *(stares at hand)*

DICKSELL:

> Now, I read all about your breakdown in the rags but hey, you don't have to talk about it now. The fact is, you're here, you've got style up the wazoo and you're prime meat for a comeback.

FRANCES:

> Comeback?

DICKSELL:

> *(stands back, points at FRANCES and says in a loud voice)*
> FRANCES FARMER, THIS IS YOUR LIFE!!!!

> *The garish set of a quiz show comes on stage. Roy Dicksell flings his hat off.*

DICKSELL:

> And I'm your host, Roy Dicksell, with a very special guest. This little lady was once a famous movie actress. She has spent the last twenty years in total obscurity—TWENTY YEARS, an unwitting victim of alcohol and drugs. She was rehabilitated and has made a remarkable COMEBACK from the depths of mental illness. So, let's give a big hand to ...FRANCES FARMER!!

> *(polite applause)*

> *FRANCES stands and stares at the quiz show set.*

DICKSELL:

> *(motions for FRANCES to come over and sit down)*

FRANCES:
    (remains where she is)

DICKSELL:
    Heh-heh-heh. I guess I'll have to go get the little lady.
    "Come and Get It" eh, Frances? *(takes FRANCES by the
    shoulders and guides her over)* Frances, you may not realize it
    but you have more friends than you know and we are
    going to take you back through your life, your triumphs
    and—

FRANCES:
    (stops in her tracks) You're going to take me back?

DICKSELL:
    Yes, Frances

FRANCES:
    I don't want to go.

DICKSELL:
    Now, Frances, it's too late to be modest. You're on national
    television.

FRANCES:
    I'm not going back there!!

VOICE OVER:
    (hushed and booming) AND THIS IS BELLE MACKENZIE—
    FRANCES' HIGH SCHOOL ENGLISH TEACHER!

    (lights up on a small old woman)

DICKSELL:
    Frances, look over there. Can you guess who that is?

FRANCES:
    No, please!

183

BELLE:

Hi, Frances. Do you remember me? I'm Belle Mackenzie.

FRANCES:

Hi, Belle. I'm sorry but I don't remember you.

BELLE:

You wrote that essay for me. "God dies."

FRANCES:

God didn't die. He's alive. You can't say those things. God didn't die!!

BELLE:

I didn't say them. You said them.

FRANCES:

No. I didn't. I could never say that. God's with me. He's with all of us. We're all faceless sinners in the sight of the Lord. *(crosses herself)* I'm a faceless sinner. I'm a faceless sinner. I'm a faceless—

DICKSELL:

GREAT! FRANCES! THAT'S GREAT!! You can stop doing that, now. AND THANKS BELLA! THANKS FOR COMING!!

BELLE:

She doesn't remember me. I came all the way from Seattle and she doesn't remember me.

DICKSELL:

All expenses paid, Bella. Can't complain.

ATTENDANTS guide BELLE off the stage.

BELLE:

BELLE! MY NAME'S BELLE!!!

FRANCES:
You're not going to bring more people to see me, are you, Roy?

DICKSELL:
Well, that was the plan.

FRANCES:
You're not going to bring my mother, are you!

DICKSELL:
Your mother died, Frances. A long time ago.

FRANCES:
Please—no more people.

Pieces of the quiz show are moved off stage with each Voice Over.

VOICE OVER:
FRANCES! EDNA BURGE IS HERE TO SEE YOU!

EDNA *(Voice Over)*:
Hi Frances. Remember when you punched me in the face. Boy, I bet you're sorry now.

VOICE OVER:
FRANCES! LOUELLA PARSONS IS HERE TO SEE YOU.

FRANCES:
NO!! PLEASE! STOP!!

VOICE OVER:
FRANCES, CLIFFORD ODETS IS HERE TO SEE YOU.

FRANCES:
AAaaah!

VOICE OVER:
  FRANCES, YOUR MOTHER IS HERE TO SEE YOU.
  SHE'S COME ALL THE WAY FROM HELL.

FRANCES:
  (screams, long, loud and bloodcurdling)

  The quiz show has left the stage. FRANCES is kneeling down, bent over and screaming. A woman (JEAN) enters. She looks like Frances' mother but she is younger and dressed in modern clothes, circa 1970. She rushes over to FRANCES and tries to comfort her.

JEAN:
  Honey, honey, stop screaming.

FRANCES:
  (stops) (gasps)

JEAN:
  You'll make your throat worse.

FRANCES:
  (hoarse voice) A nightmare.

      * NOTE:
      FRANCES voice is the same sort of hoarseness that you get with laryngitis. It is HOARSE.

JEAN:
  It's all right, honey. You're with me.

FRANCES:
  Too many people. Don't know who they are. *(looks at JEAN)* Don't know who you are.

JEAN:
  I guess I've been asking you too many questions.

FRANCES:

Jean? Is that you?

JEAN:

Yes. It's me. Are you seeing faces again?

FRANCES:

You look like my mother.

JEAN:

Now, that's not a nice thing to say, dear. I'm not at all like your mother.

FRANCES:

I bet you are. My throat's sore.

JEAN:

You shouldn't scream, dear. It upsets the cancer.

FRANCES:

What's cancer?

JEAN:

Honey, we've been through this. It's a disease. You've got a disease in your throat and you're going to die. But don't worry. I've almost finished the story of your life.

FRANCES:

Whose life?

JEAN:

Yours. Why don't we say a little bedtime prayer and chase those bad dreams away.

FRANCES:

I'm glad I found God, Jean.

JEAN:

God's glad you found Him, too. You're His little angel.

FRANCES:

Jean, if we pray really hard, do you think God will give me back my brains?

JEAN:

God loves you just the way you are.

FRANCES:

I know.

JEAN:

(puts FRANCES in kneeling position) Gentle Jesus, meek and mild—

FRANCES:

Can we say the other one?

JEAN:

You can never remember that one.

FRANCES:

Can we say it, anyway?

JEAN:

All right. *(hurriedly)* "The Lord is my shepherd I shall not want."

FRANCES:

The Lord is my shepherd I shall not want.

JEAN:

He maketh me...

FRANCES:

(looks at JEAN blankly)

JEAN:

He maketh me to lie down in green pastures
He leadeth me beside the still waters.

FRANCES:
   He restoreth my soul.

JEAN:
   Very good, Frances.

FRANCES:
   He restoreth my soul.

JEAN:
   Yes. Now, what's next?

FRANCES:
   (shouts) HE RESTORETH MY SOUL!

   *Lights change suddenly—go out—flash spotlight on
   FRANCES. Lights come back on but there is an odd quality
   to the lighting. It is blue and eerie. FRANCES stares down at
   her hands. The palms are glowing slightly. JEAN does not
   notice FRANCES' hands.*

JEAN:
   That's odd.

FRANCES:
   Jean, I feel funny. *(touches one of her hands to her head)*

JEAN:
   Oh no, is it time? Do you want me to go get the kittens? So
   you can hold them?

FRANCES:
   I hate cats.

JEAN:
   Don't be silly, Frances. You love cats.

FRANCES:
   No. You love cats. I hate them.

JEAN:

Do you want to play with Sport, instead?

FRANCES:

(looks at her)

JEAN:

The dog. Sport the dog.

FRANCES:

(withering contempt) Sport?

JEAN:

Yes. You like Sport. Go play with Sport.

FRANCES:

Something is happening to my head. *(clutches her head)* Jean, why do you think I had such a rotten life?

JEAN:

God was punishing you because you didn't believe in Him.

FRANCES:

But I believe now and He's given me cancer.

JEAN:

The cancer is a punishment for all those bad things you said about Him in the past. Frances? You don't sound yourself.

FRANCES:

Do you think I'm dying?

JEAN:

(brushes FRANCES' hair with her hand) Yes. *(sobs)*

FRANCES:

Good.

JEAN:
    What?

FRANCES:
    I want to die.

JEAN:
    Oh, of course, dear. The pain must be unbearable.

FRANCES:
    It's not the pain, Jean. It's you.

JEAN:
    What?

FRANCES:
    It's you. It's my mother. It's this country. It's God. It's
    everyone who put me through this fucking shithole of a
    life and I am fucking getting out!

JEAN:
    FRANCES! STOP THAT! STOP THAT THIS INSTANT!!

FRANCES:
    I am fucking leaving. For good. And this time, no one's
    going to stop me. And you can take your fucking kittens
    and your fucking dog named Sport...

JEAN:
    WHAT'S THE MATTER WITH YOU!! HAVE YOU GONE
    MAD!

FRANCES:
    AND YOUR FUCKING BIOGRAPHY AND SHOVE IT UP
    YOUR FUCKING ASS!!! *(dies)*

THE END

191

Stage Mock-up for "Stellacoom Hospital"
Saint Frances of Hollywood by Sally Clark

Design : Adam Swica © 1996

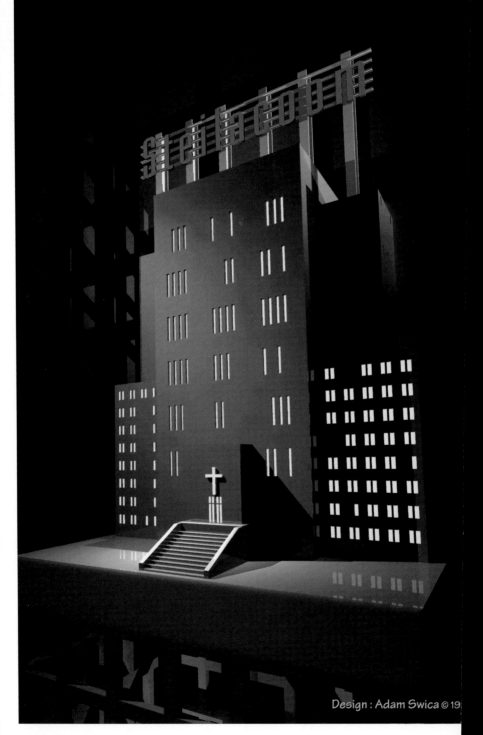

Design : Adam Swica © 19

ЛЕНИН

Design : Adam Swica © 1996

Design : Randy Gledhill
Illustration : Adam Swica ©199

La Cresenta

SCREEN ACTORS SANITURIUM

HOLLYWOODLAND